YOUR UCAS PERSONAL STATEMENT

WHAT TO WRITE IF YOU WANT TO GET IN

for Business, Economics, Finance, Management & Accounting

by

Gwyn Day and Chloë Daniel

Published by gwynday.com, UK

ISBN: 978-0-9926649-6-1

CONTENTS

INTRODUCTION

MY BACKGROUND

I am an educational coach specialising in beating admissions procedures. With 20 years of experience, I know what university admissions tutors are looking for. My expertise is in helping you give them what they want to win your place at your chosen university.

This is why the top fee-paying schools in the country (where parents pay annual fees of over £35,000) bring me in to talk to their students; it is why I am on the Supervisory Board of Oxbridge Applications and deliver training sessions to thousands of students every year; and it is why I am flown to India, Dubai, and Hong Kong to prepare individual private clients for their university and job applications.

The people I help fall into three main groups:

Group 1: Students who want to get into the best university possible given their grade profile.

Group 2: Students with excellent grade profiles who want to get into Oxford, Cambridge, Medical School, or US Ivy League colleges.

Group 3: Undergraduates who want careers in Investment Banking, Management Consultancy, or Law (focusing on getting Vacation Scheme placements and Training Contracts). For more details, see “The Programme” on my website www.gwynday.com and the book “Gwyn and The City - Commercial Awareness for Future Bankers, Lawyers, and Management Consultants”.

If you are reading this book, the chances are you fall into **Group 1** or **Group 2**. Welcome! Now let’s move on to getting you into a great university.

Getting an offer from good universities depends on four (and sometimes more) factors:

1. Your GCSE grade profile (too late to worry about that)
2. Your AS results and predicted grades (that’s your job)
3. Your Teacher's Reference (see Chapter 11)
4. Your Personal Statement - read on ...
5. Some universities require admissions tests, interviews, and submitted work (see Chapter 14)

Here is some great news. If you follow all the guidance in this book, you will get an offer from one of your five chosen universities (providing your AS grades match the university’s requirements).

This book will help you write your own exceptional Personal Statement. Some students are looking for more one-on-one support. If you want me to advise, correct, edit, and proofread your Personal Statement unlimited times until you are happy with it, contact me via www.gwynday.com to arrange a chat.

YOUR PERSONAL STATEMENT

Let's start with the basics. Your Personal Statement is part of your UCAS application and is submitted online along with your personal details, grade profile, and university choices.

For your Personal Statement, UCAS gives you 4,000 characters (including spaces). This roughly equates to one side of A4 paper. That is one side of paper to give the admissions tutors at your chosen universities enough evidence to show that you are smart, genuinely interested in your subject, understand the demands and benefits of the course, will contribute to the university, and ... that you can write coherent, accurate, structured English.

A daunting prospect? This is much more straightforward than it sounds. The secret to success is knowing how to give the admissions tutors what they want - that means knowing how to match their idea of a great candidate.

My expert advice tells you how to do just that. With suggested reading, example paragraphs, practice exercises, and the lowdown on the main errors students make, the logical and detailed steps in this book will guide you through writing an exceptional Personal Statement that puts you ahead of the competition.

Follow all of the advice and you will get in. Do not cut corners.

PLAGIARISM ALERTS

Throughout the book you will see the following warning written above sections that you are most likely to want to copy directly into your Personal Statement.

****PLAGIARISM ALERT****

Universities have plagiarism software to compare Personal Statements submitted this year with a huge database of those from previous years. This book, and others similar, will be scanned and added to their database. <u>If you copy, you will be caught</u>.

Help is at hand. Chapter 9 takes you through the different phrases, tweaks to word order, and bigger structural changes you can use to make your Personal Statement truly <u>yours</u>. This means that you get to use all the ideas in this book and still finish with a unique and effective Personal Statement.

FAQs

Question 1: When should I start writing my Personal Statement?

The best time to <u>finalise</u> your Personal Statement is immediately after your AS (or equivalent) results come in. By waiting until you get your AS (or equivalent) results, you will know which universities and courses will be relevant for you. It is all about being realistic. If your results are lower than expected, it will not make sense to apply to universities with a high grade threshold. If your grades are better than expected, you may want to change your target universities.

The period earlier in the summer, between finishing your AS exams and getting your results, is still crucially important. This is the perfect time to get your Personal Statement research done and start writing initial drafts.

Most universities offer places on a rolling basis. By submitting your UCAS application early you increase your chances of getting the offer you want. In reality, that means you must aim to submit your completed application long before the deadline (15th October for Oxbridge, Medicine, Dentistry, and Veterinary Medicine, and 15th January for all other university courses).

I strongly advise completing your Personal Statement before the A2 year starts in September. Most students massively underestimate the A2 workload, and having to write your Personal Statement from draft 1, while staying on top of your school work, is extremely difficult (though it can be done).

The Personal Statement Timeline in Chapter 1 shows you exactly what to do and when.

(NOTE: If you decide to work with me on your Personal Statement one-on-one, we can start the process as soon as your exams are over. You get unlimited rewrites and checks, and, by starting early, I can guide you through the initial research.)

Question 2: How many drafts will it take to get my Personal Statement right?

If you want to produce a truly outstanding Personal Statement, in my experience you will be close to a final version within seven to ten drafts. Once you think you are close to a final version, you will realise one of two things. Either (1) you are well over the 4,000 character count and do not know what to take out because "it's all important", or (2) you have written more than half of your statement on extracurricular activities instead of detailing why you are the right candidate for your chosen course. Chapter 11 helps you fix these sorts of mistakes and turn your draft into its final, successful version.

Question 3: How much time will it take me to write it?

Much longer than you think. Writing time will add up to somewhere between ten and twelve hours. Before that, you will need time for research, extra reading, and online lectures, which, if done properly, could take you two to three days. Students considering Oxbridge and Russell Group universities should factor in at least two or three more hours for writing, plus an additional day for research. The good news is that using this book will significantly reduce the amount of time required and give you a much better finished product.

Question 4: Where do I start?

"I don't know how to start" is the most common concern I hear when working with students in schools, so you are not alone. Chapters 4, 5, 9, and 10 give specific ideas and phrase suggestions to get you started.

Question 5: How do I know when my Personal Statement is finished?

As with any carefully crafted piece of writing, your Personal Statement is never finished. You can keep on replacing a word here or there, tweaking the word order, or finding another lecture or book that fits in with your interests. You must go for "optimum" rather than perfect.

Follow the advice in this book and your Personal Statement will be excellent. Then move on: concentrate on getting the grades at A2, and, for those of you who have them, excelling at interviews and admissions tests.

Question 6: I cannot fit in everything I want to say. How do I choose?

The art of writing an excellent Personal Statement is in choosing what is most directly relevant to demonstrate (not describe) your interest in your subject. Chapters 4, 5, 6, 7, and 8 take you through how to decide what is relevant and what is not.

Once you have established what you want to say, you then need to trim the word count. The exercises in Chapter 11 show you how to reduce the length of your statement without losing valuable content.

Remember a Personal Statement showing subject-specific reading and relevant, subject-specific activities, with only two lines on your “other hobbies”, is fine. Writing half (or more) of your Personal Statement on playing football and your band’s latest gig is not.

Question 7: I am applying for slightly different courses at different universities - how do I deal with that?

Though many students feel apprehensive about tackling this challenge, the solution is straightforward. The trick is identifying the common ground between the different courses, and then providing enough strong evidence of your suitability for these shared elements to show that you will be a great candidate for each of your choices.

Question 8: I do not have any evidence to show why I am interested in the course. What should I do?

You are set for a busy summer, but, if you are applying for a subject which genuinely interests you, the process of accumulating this evidence (though time-consuming) will be fun. To set about this as efficiently as possible, it is essential you read Chapters 4, 5, and 6 thoroughly. They detail easy ways to expand your reading and activities, and then how to work this evidence of your interest and motivation into your Personal Statement.

Being selective is key - otherwise you will be overwhelmed by new information. From my lists of suggestions (in Chapters 4, 5, and 6) pick only:

- two books (Chapter 4);
- three lectures from either TED or iTunes U (Chapter 5);
- one piece of archived material from the listed societies (e.g. Royal Society or Intelligence Squared) (Chapter 5).

Rather than overfilling your head with more information, take time to analyse and compare your selection cleverly. Do this, and you will be fine.

(NOTE: If this is your situation, I strongly advise using my One-on-One Personal Statement Coaching. See www.gwynday.com for details.)

Question 9: I am applying for a course I have not studied at Sixth Form. What am I supposed to say?

Many students face the same challenge and it is an easy one to deal with. Chapters 2, 4, and 5 give you all you need to know on how.

Question 10: I do not know why I want to study my chosen course - I just do. What do I write then?

If you feel like this, you need to follow this book to the word. The examples given will provide you with many possible approaches and routes to take. Choose the approach which attracts you the most and you feel most comfortable with. Springboard off the examples given - especially in Chapters 4 and 5. By the end, you will definitely have some great reasons for your choice.

Question 11: I want my Personal Statement to be unique. I'm worried it will be too formulaic if I use this book.

There are only so many things that can be said in a Personal Statement (give me £1 for every time I read about Duke of Edinburgh's Awards or Grade 8 violin). A strong Personal Statement is more about the "how" than the "what". For good candidates, the "what" (e.g. books, activities, hobbies) is likely to be fairly constant. Most people do A-levels (or an equivalent), read around their subject, and have a few hobbies.

What differs is "how" you go about your Personal Statement. Have you given evidence rather than describing what you do? Have you been specific? Have you used a varied and intelligent writing style, and taken the time to ensure your Personal Statement is free of errors? These are the things that make a Personal Statement stand out.

The exercises in Chapters 9 and 11 will help you turn your strong "core" Personal Statement into a captivating and unique one.

Question 12: My teachers and others are giving different advice to you. Who is right?

Many great teachers, Heads of Sixth, and Careers Advisors know this process inside out. Look at the success rate certain schools have in getting their students into the top universities. Others do not, and that goes for parents too. They want to "help" but can sometimes end up causing confusion and weakening your application.

When you go to Open Days at your target universities or if admissions tutors visit your school, listen closely to what they say. Read all the free Personal Statement advice you can find online. Then compare it to what I say and decide for yourself. Ultimately, it is your Personal Statement.

Question 13: You mentioned that if my AS results are lower than expected I should avoid applying to certain universities because their grade thresholds are too high. I am confident that I can improve at A2. Can I write my Personal Statement on that basis?

There are two reasons why it is rare (though not impossible) for students to significantly improve on their AS results at A2: (1) A2 exams are much tougher than AS; and (2) the weighting of the marks allocated in AS/A2 makes it much easier to do well at AS.

For the vast majority of students I see, it is much more realistic to apply on the basis of AS results. If you do end up markedly improving at A2, you can always take a gap year and apply again the following year.

Question 14: I would like to work with you directly. What do I do?

Contact me via my website (www.gwynday.com), and I will be in touch to discuss rates and timeframes.

Chapter 1

PERSONAL STATEMENT TIMELINES

You are probably reading this book because you have just finished your AS exams and your teachers want you to start working on UCAS and your university application. The exact date you start this process will vary from school to school. To make it clear, I have set out a sequential timeline without fixed dates. This serves as a set of steps to follow from the moment you start.

Very few students will plan so far ahead that they are reading this earlier in Year 12, but if you are, see the "Ideal Timeline" at the end of this chapter.

SEQUENTIAL TIMELINE

Step 1

Read this book all the way through and make no notes.

Step 2

Read the book again.

Step 3

According to the different examples given in the chapters (e.g. books, lectures, extracurricular activities), make a list of everything you have done or been involved in so far which could be relevant for your statement.

Step 4

Identify the gaps. By that I mean work out what additional material you need to fully prove your suitability for your chosen course (e.g. one or two articles in subject-related magazines; a few TED talks or archived university public lectures; relevant work experience for the summer holidays).

Step 5

Complete or set up the extra work you identified in Step 4.

Step 6

Research your chosen courses and universities. Make notes about particular modules, course structure, opportunities (e.g. dissertation; time abroad; career opportunities), and the specific qualities they are looking for in candidates.

Step 7

Using the relevant chapters of this book to guide you, draft each paragraph of your Personal Statement in turn. It is fine for what you write to be rough at this stage; you will go on to revise each section many times. Your main focus here is getting your information down.

Step 8

Re-read the chapters relevant to each paragraph and use the information to improve the phrasing and particular words in your statement.

Step 9
Check your statement for "banned language", bad style, and overused clichés, as highlighted in Chapter 3, and replace with better expressions.

Step 10
Use Chapter 9 to edit, restructure, and refine your Personal Statement until you are confident that it feels truly yours.

Step 11
Check the length of your statement. Use Chapter 11 to make it more concise and to weed out any final errors. Then complete this process again.

Step 12
Ask someone else to check the content and look for potential errors you have missed. Bear in mind, however, that you are going to receive advice from many sources (this book, teachers, your parents / guardians, university tutors coming into school, even online forums). Ultimately, you decide. It is your Personal Statement, nobody else's. Choose from all the advice and use what is right for you.

IDEAL TIMELINE

If you have got yourself organised early in Year 12, or even in the summer between GCSEs and AS, you have lots of time to ensure you have all the evidence you need to write a truly outstanding Personal

Statement. The following calendar timeline will guide you through the process.

1. Year 12: September / October

Start building evidence of your interest and motivation by:
(a) researching universities & courses;
(b) joining relevant clubs and societies at, or outside of, school;
(c) reading books and making notes;
(d) attending free public lectures and watching lectures online.

2. Year 12: March

Use this book to write the first draft of your Personal Statement. During this process, identify what gaps of knowledge or experience you still need to fill.

3. Year 12: April / May

Revise - doing your absolute best in your AS exams is the most important thing right now.

4. Year 12: June, post-AS exams

Write draft 2 of your Personal Statement.

5. Year 12: June / July

Attend Open Days at the universities you are considering.

6. Year 12: July / August

Refine the material already in your statement and move towards a final draft.

(a) Work in relevant summer activity (e.g. summer schools, latest books, current affairs).
(b) Prepare for admissions tests and potential interviews.
(c) Check character count.
(d) Use the "Style Guide" in Chapter 3 to make sure your statement reads as fluently as possible.
(e) Check the proportion of subject-specific material is enough.

7. Year 13: September 30th

Final internal deadline, either for school or for you.

8. Year 13: October 15th

Oxbridge, Medicine, Dentistry, and Veterinary Medicine deadline.

9. Year 13: December 1st

Absolute last advised deadline for any non-Oxbridge / Medicine applications.

10. Year 13: January 15th

Actual UCAS submission deadline.

Chapter 2

GETTING STARTED: PERSONAL STATEMENT OVERVIEW

Before you start writing your Personal Statement, or even doing the background research, it helps to have a sense of the basic structure you will use. Knowing what information you are ultimately aiming to include, and in what order, gives you an idea of where each paragraph is going and the purpose of your research.

BASIC STRUCTURE

Your Personal Statement will consist of five paragraphs. At this early drafting stage, the five paragraph structure ensures that you include everything necessary to produce a robust final Personal Statement. Tweaks and styling can come later.

When you finally submit your statement via UCAS, it will flow as one single block of text. Doing otherwise is impossible because of the 4,000 characters limit. Despite this, you will still think of your statement in terms of clear paragraphs, each addressing a specific point.

Chapters 4, 5, 6, 7, and 8 in this book each tackle a separate paragraph, taking you through how to pull together and present the relevant material. Chapter 9 shows you how to give your Personal Statement the emphasis and narrative most important to you.

Paragraph 1: Why this course

Admissions tutors want to you to prove that you are motivated to study your chosen course and that you have reflected on and understand why you want to study it. The five “big reasons" you can give are in Chapter 4. Whichever reason you decide on, ultimately important is showing that you have given solid thought to your decision.

Paragraph 2: Examples of subject-specific further reading (i.e. not part of your obligatory A-level work)

Having evidence of your interest in your subject beyond your A-level work is absolutely essential. This is how you can make your Personal Statement shine out among the many mediocre ones. You go to university to read a subject, so no surprise that you get bonus points for talking intelligently about reading you have done off your own back at Sixth Form.

If you have not yet done any wider reading, Chapter 5 gives you plenty of ideas on where to start, including specific examples of books to mention in your statement and quotes you can use. Just referencing two or three books related to your areas of interest will put you far ahead of most candidates.

Paragraph 3: Other <u>subject-specific</u> extracurricular activities

Getting involved in activities related to a subject you are interested in is easy. Showing how these experiences have deepened or sharpened your understanding of your subject - what admissions tutors expect - requires more thought. Chapter 6 takes you through how to do this effectively.

Paragraph 4: <u>Non subject-specific</u> extracurricular activities

There are multiple options to include here. Sports at international / national / county / school level; music; drama; having a part-time job; hobbies; Duke of Edinburgh's Award; School Council; Head Boy; Head Girl; Prefect; raising money for charity, the list goes on ...

With so many options, many students get it wrong by writing a shopping list of their achievements. This is simply not relevant for admissions tutors. Instead, you need to show how these activities are relevant for the skills required at university and, more specifically, for your course. Chapter 7 gives you ideas on what to include and how to present these to prove that you have what it takes.

Paragraph 5: Wrap up

In the fifth and final paragraph of your Personal Statement you will talk about what you want to gain from your degree and where you want it to take you (e.g. career / postgraduate study). Adding a personal comment that comes "from the heart" is a nice touch; so do mention, for example, that you are the first person in your family to go to university, that your family recently moved to the UK, or that English is your second language.

(NOTE 1: The first three paragraphs should make up approximately 75% of your Personal Statement (that equates to 3,000 characters including spaces).)

(NOTE 2: Teachers often instruct students to include details of what they have learned in their A-levels. Personally, I think (and the success of my clients has proven) that concentrating on evidence (of research, interest, ability, competence) rather than giving a descriptive statement regarding A-level content is much more effective in impressing admissions tutors. The examples below show you why.)

Example -- okay but not ideal:

My four subjects at AS level have been very useful: Maths for logic and problem-solving, Geography for an understanding of how different forces work together, Chemistry for practical laboratory skills, and Economics for the ability to evaluate data-rich material objectively.

Example -- much better:

This degree course, according to your prospectus, values skills such as data evaluation and problem-solving. The former is shown by my EPQ on "Property Prices in Las Vegas 2006 - 2014", which looked at geopolitical and macroeconomic forces, whilst also factoring in local pressures. My gold medals in two Maths Olympiads evidence the latter.

(NOTE 3: The situation is slightly different if you are applying for a subject <u>not</u> studied at A-level (or equivalent), such as Accounting or Actuarial Studies. In this instance, you need to refer to your A-levels to show that the skills you have learned in your school subjects and through any relevant extracurricular activities are transferable to your chosen university course.)

Example -- good:

“A degree in Actuarial Studies will draw upon the strong skills I have developed from several of my A-level subjects. Maths and Further Maths give me the quantitative literacy required. Physics and Chemistry involve the practical application of Mathematics which Actuarial Studies aims to achieve.”

Chapter 3

STYLE GUIDE

Expressing yourself intelligently is one of the best ways to make your Personal Statement stand out. To achieve this, thinking carefully about the style of writing you will use, before you start, is crucial.

The vast majority of the statements I see, including from top Oxbridge candidates, employ the same set of unimaginative stock phrases and fall into some very predictable language traps. Avoid these in yours and you will be far ahead of the competition.

Below I have highlighted the worst offenders. From now on consider these "banned style" and "banned words" to strictly avoid in your Personal Statement. Using the suggested alternatives will make a much better first impression with admissions tutors.

BANNED STYLE

1: Starting with a quote

Starting your Personal Statement with a quote is unimaginative and fails to show the admissions tutors anything other than your ability to use Google. Your Personal Statement is about why <u>you</u> want to do the course, not about some business guru, philosopher, or novelist.

Quotes can be appropriate elsewhere in your statement - see the examples in Chapter 5 (which guides you through writing paragraph 2). For this all important first line, however, a sentence about you and your motivation is much more effective.

A few of the worst offenders ...

Law	"Laws are like cobwebs, which may catch small flies, but let wasps and hornets break through." (Jonathan Swift)
Physics	"Photons have mass? I didn't even know they were Catholic." (Woody Allen)
English	"She'd become an English major for the purest and dullest of reasons: because she loved to read." (Jeffrey Eugenides, The Marriage Plot)
Business	"Sometimes when you innovate, you make mistakes. It is best to admit them quickly, and get on with improving your other innovations." (Steve Jobs)
Finance	"Capital isn't scare; vision is." (Sam Walton, Founder of Walmart)
Economics	"If all the economists were laid end to end, they'd never reach a conclusion." George Bernard Shaw
Accounting	"Make every detail perfect and limit the number of details to perfect." (Jack Dorsey, Twitter Co-Founder)

2: Describing

The purpose of your Personal Statement is to convince admissions tutors of your interest in and aptitude for your chosen subject. Using what you know and have done to show your suitability is much more interesting to them than a long-winded regurgitation of the university prospectus, your A-level syllabus, or a random list of your achievements. Clear points plus evidence is key.

Example -- not so good:

"Economics is a multidisciplinary subject looking at both the macro and micro. Really it's about the allocation of resources." (So what. The tutor knows all of this and it says nothing about you.)

Example -- better:

"The multidisciplinary aspect of Economics, particularly Macroeconomics and Econometrics, appeals to me as I can develop skills in ..."

3: Poetry

At best, overly flowery language is a waste of precious space, especially if combined with describing (see above). At worst, it makes you sound pretentious.

Examples -- not so good:

"The Law is a river which runs through the land of England feeding and nourishing the people."

“I am a passionate Geography student and am fond of exploring the majestic landscapes of South America.”

Examples -- better:

“The ubiquity of Law and the multiplicity of interpretations are key attractions to studying this subject at university.”

“Exploring the Pantanal in South America and researching potential medical uses for plants (such as [XYZ]) reinforced the importance of conservation.”

4: Egoism

Convince tutors that you are someone they want to teach, not someone so overconfident that you might not be willing to learn. Tell it like it is and always emphasise the relevance of your achievements for your course.

Example -- not so good:

"My great success at the Physics Olympiad, winning a gold medal for the second year running, shows that I am right for this course."

Example -- better:

"Working hard and independently preparing for the Physics Olympiad was rewarding, especially when I won the gold medal (for the second year,) and gives a good foundation for university-level work."

5: Extreme sentencing

Clear writing comes from clear thinking. If you find yourself writing in long, complicated sentences, it is likely that you have not yet worked out exactly what it is you want to say. Take a moment to think before you start writing to be sure of the purpose of each sentence. Then make your writing as concise as you can and punctuate properly (see Chapter 11).

Example -- not so good:

"Learning about "mavens" in Gladwell's "The Tipping Point" showed me the importance for many different kinds of business of first establishing a small and devoted group of customers, who are willing to go out and evangelise a product or service, as a sustainable way of growing a larger customer base and having read Isaacson's biography of Steve Jobs I could see that this is where much of Apple's early business success came from."

Example -- better:

"Gladwell's "mavens" in "The Tipping Point" show how businesses must establish a solid and devoted customer base. A good example of this is how Apple's decision to appeal to "the crazy ones" in an early advert contributed to their initial popularity. This combination of psychology and innovation in Marketing appeals to me; and I have already applied the "mavens" principle successfully to market my start-up's handprinted T-shirts to other students."

6: Phrase / word repetition

So many of the statements I review use the same phrase over and over again. It makes the ideas sound dull, even if they are not. Common offenders are:

- "led me to"
- "allowed me to"
- "gave me an understanding of"
- "gave me an insight into"

Carefully review what you have written, and where you see repetition use synonyms (see the examples in Chapter 9). You are smart, you are going to study at university, so show your range of vocabulary.

7: Using “one” instead of “I” and “my”

This sounds pretentious. “I” and “my” are much more engaging.

Example -- not so good:

“Reading broadly to improve one’s knowledge of the classics of English literature ...”

Example -- better:

“Reading Thomas Mann’s “Buddenbrooks” and Tolstoy’s “War and Peace” has helped me see the great English novels in the context of a wider nineteenth-century European literary movement.”

8: Subject abuse

Frequent use of “I” at the start of a sentence can make you sound big-headed (and repetitive).

- “I gained” / “I developed” / “I learnt” / “I joined” / “I took part in” / “I lead” / etc.

Using gerunds (a verb plus “ing”) at the start of sentences is psychologically more active, saves characters, and, most importantly, gives that bounce and enthusiasm that admission tutors are looking for in a Personal Statement.

Example -- better:

"Leading the school's Finance Society has given me a better understanding of what it takes to market an event - specifically how to appeal to my target customers. This is an area of Business I would like to learn more about at university level."

9. Being overly chatty

Your Personal Statement is a piece of serious academic writing, not a Facebook message to a friend.

Example -- not so good:

"My Aunt Lisa, who has worked in hospitals most of her life ... "

Example -- better:

"Discussing NHS management challenges with relatives who have worked in the medical field for many years ..."

10: Exclamation marks

Just do not use them. Not one! Certainly not more!!!

11: Abbreviations

Whether referring to a school society or an aspect of the economy, what you are writing about may be obvious to you but not to admissions tutors.

Example -- not so good:

"Taking part in the USBC summer school / Whitgift SNAP has developed ..."

Example -- better:

"Taking part in a local charity (Whitgift SNAP) involved organising a Summer Fair with a group of volunteers and developed my communication skills and rapport-building."

12: Starting a sentence with "And"

This is a stylistic preference rather than a grammatical rule. Though not wrong as such, the expression is best left in fiction writing, where you might be aiming for dramatic effect, not your Personal Statement.

Example -- not so good:

"And, reading George Osborne's speech to the House of Commons following the 2014 budget underlined for me how economic policy is often motivated by a political agenda."

Example -- better:

"George Osborne's speech following the 2014 Budget served to further emphasise how economic policy is strongly influenced by the current political agenda."

13: Starting a sentence with "But"

As above, this is not grammatically incorrect, but many people do not like it (especially English teachers and admissions tutors). The additional risk in using this construction is that it creates a sense of surprise you probably did not intend to convey.

Example -- not so good:

"Reading about the practical application of business theory in large corporations is fascinating. But, since starting my own business, I have seen how even small improvements, such as reducing customer acquisition cost by 20%, can make a big difference to the bottom line."

Example -- better:

"Having read in the Financial Times that [XYZ] company reduced customer acquisition costs by 20% by focusing on their most effective marketing channels only, I applied this same theory to my own business selling t-shirts in school and have successfully increased my profit figures.

BANNED WORDS

1: "to be able"

This is a waste of characters. The examples below show why.

Example -- not so good:

"By completing the Duke of Edinburgh's Gold Award I was able to improve my communication skills and ability to organise myself."

Examples -- better:

"By completing the Duke of Edinburgh's Gold Award I improved my communication skills and ability to organise myself."

"My communication and organisational skills, both vital for degree-level study, have been significantly improved by completing the Duke of Edinburgh's Gold Award."

2: "had to"

Another way to waste characters; compare the examples below.

Example -- not so good:

"Running the Biology Society at school meant I had to organise several guest speakers and motivate students to give short talks. "

Example -- better:

"Running the Biology Society at school meant organising several guest speakers and motivating students to give short talks."

3: "relish"

Relish belongs on burgers - with cheese!

Example - not so good:

"I would relish the opportunity to study Chemistry at degree level."

Example -- better:

"Studying Chemistry for the next three years is what I want to do because it enables me to study [XYZ] in detail and then pursue a career as a Research Scientist."

4: “thrive”

Write this about plants growing in your back garden, not about yourself at university. Prove that university will be the right place for you by giving evidence instead.

Example -- not so good:

“I thrive on hard work.”

Examples -- better:

"Self-studying an extra AS-level demonstrates my willingness to commit to do what is necessary to achieve my goals.” (Giving an example of how you thrive on hard work)

"Choosing to do an EPQ in addition to four A-levels evidences my ability to prioritise and meet multiple deadlines, which will be useful skills at university.” (As above)

5: “passion” and “desire”

Neither of these words proves your interest in your subject. Let me say it again: expressions like this are empty - only specific examples show that you are passionate about your subject.

Examples -- not so good:

"My passion for Business confirms I want to do this as a degree and in my future career."

"My desire to study Medicine springs from a childhood incident when I had to spend ten weeks in hospital ..."

Examples -- better:

"I have researched the intensity of study in this Business course through talking to current students at Open Days, family, friends, and people on graduate trainee schemes in big companies. The idea of putting theory into practice on a daily basis is one of the main draws of this degree and to a career in this field."

"Ten weeks in hospital at a young age gave me my first understanding of multidisciplinary teamwork in Medicine."

6: "also" and "too"

This is a Personal Statement, not a shopping list. Chapter 7 tells you in detail how to present your many extracurricular activities without falling into the "also" trap.

Example -- not so good:

"I am a Prefect at my school and <u>also</u> on the football, rugby, and cricket teams. I am active in several local charities <u>too</u>."

Example -- better:

"Combining the responsibilities of a Prefect and playing on multiple sports teams has proven my ability to effectively prioritise and plan my time, both of which are vital for successful study at university level."

7: "In addition" or "Additionally" at the start of a sentence

Another shopping list trap.

Example -- not so good:

"In addition, I play county-level netball and I am captain of the school hockey team."

Example -- better:

"Playing county-level netball and captaining the school hockey team have developed teamwork skills which will help with the group projects required in this degree."

8: "However" or "Moreover" at the start of a sentence

Again, neither is grammatically incorrect (though many people believe them to be). You probably use one or both all the time in your school essays. Correct or not, these formulations are clumsy and use up unnecessary character count. My advice - avoid.

Example -- not so good:

"However, when we look at Carr's "What is History"..."

Examples -- better:

"Looking at Carr's "What is History" ... "

"Carr's "What is History" shows us that ... "

9: "lucky enough"

This is too informal and adds nothing to enhance the meaning of the sentence.

Example -- not so good:

"I was lucky enough to gain work experience with a Senior Consultant at [XY] Hospital and observed several cases including [XYZ]."

(This gives the impression that your mother / father / uncle works at the hospital and either arranged your work experience for you or is actually the Senior Consultant.)

Example -- better:

"Researching the causes, symptoms, and treatments for [XYZ] resulted from observing a patient with this condition during my work experience with a Senior Consultant at [XY] Hospital."

10: "really"

Sentences with "really" use extra words to describe rather than demonstrate. Using creative ways to emphasise something you feel or think intensely will better show your ability to write well.

Examples -- not so good:

"I want to study Mathematics at university because I really enjoy it."

"I get really involved in activities at school, especially in Geography."

"I have really, really pushed myself to understand more about glaciation."

Examples -- better:

“What I enjoy about studying Mathematics is breaking problems into logical steps.”

“Doing Geography at school has taught me the importance of accuracy and attention to detail when doing fieldwork.”

“Wanting to understand more about glaciation led me to read two papers by the British Arctic Survey team.”

11: “in order to”

Another clumsy formulation which uses up precious characters. With the help of the examples below and some thought, find a way to rephrase your thoughts more economically.

Example -- not so good:

“I have taken Additional Mathematics in order to make the Econometrics and Statistical Modelling papers in the first two years of the degree easier to handle.”

Example -- better:

“Taking Additional Mathematics as an extra A-level was a conscious choice to make the Econometrics and Statistical Modelling papers in the first two years of the degree easier.”

12: "always"

No-one has always loved a particular academic subject. Writing this does not prove your aptitude for the subject, nor does it give evidence of how you have proactively pursued your interest beyond your academic work. Prove your interest with detailed examples instead.

Example -- not so good:

"I have always loved Economics."

Example -- better:

"Learning about [XYZ] aspect of macroeconomic theory at AS-level, which I found fascinating, spurred me to negotiate an improved supplier contract for my start-up business doing [ABC] and increase profitability by [X]%."

Chapter 4

Personal Statement Paragraph 1: WHY THIS COURSE?

It is time to turn theory into practice and start putting your ideas down on paper. By the end of this chapter you will know what you are going to write in Paragraph 1 - the all important opener to your Personal Statement - and have a first draft.

Here, you will tell the admissions tutors exactly why you want to study your chosen subject. If you are not yet clear on why, there are multiple ideas below to serve as a prompt. If you are already clear on why, this advice will help you formulate your reason(s) effectively.

Simply stating the reason(s) for your interest is not enough; you must find evidence to prove it. The more personal your statement, the more convincing it will be. That means my suggestions should be a stimulus for some deep thought and reflection before you start writing.

FIVE SUGGESTED REASONS

Reason 1 and 2: You love it and want to study it in more depth

There are two aspects to this statement and you must make sure you address both. Firstly, you are saying that you have a specific area of interest (within one of your A-levels or from extracurricular reading), which you want to find out more about at university. Secondly, you are acknowledging that, to go into this specific area properly, you must first improve your elementary understanding of the subject.

In fact, many degrees clearly specify that the first two years are designed to give you a broad general understanding of the subject. If this is true for your chosen course, be sure to reference it.

Before you start, you must check:

(a) All five of your chosen universities have modules covering the specialisation you are talking about.

(b) In relation to this specialist area you have done at least two of the following:
- written on it (EPQ / competitions / blog - see Chapter 6);
- read about it (books / magazines / websites - see Chapter 5);
- attended lectures (public lectures / guest speakers at school / online TED Talks or iTunesU / summer schools / taster days - see Chapter 6).

****PLAGIARISM ALERT****

Example:

"I am looking to gain a broad understanding of [your subject] before learning in more detail about [your specialist area], which I wrote on in my EPQ and which interests me most, in my third year.

Reason 3: Specific trigger

This reason is often overdone by students, but when used well can be very effective. As mentioned in Chapter 3 in the "banned words" section, nobody has "always" loved their subject. There must have been something which triggered your interest. For example:

(a) a trip / visit;
(b) a teacher;
(c) a module in your AS course;
(d) a book you read;
(e) a lecture you attended / listened to (see Chapter 6);
(f) personal / family experience.

Having worked out which event or experience it was, you then need to express how this acted as a catalyst for you to find out more about the subject and, at a later stage, to research what doing it at degree level would entail. See the examples at the end of this chapter.

Reason 4: You are good at it

People are usually good at subjects they like, and like subjects they are good at. This is a perfectly adequate reason for wanting to study a subject at university. The key is introducing evidence to prove this rather than just stating it as fact. Talking about GCSE grades will not be enough.

Reason 5: Career

University professors are professors because they love their subject for its own sake, not because it is a stepping stone to something else. That said, many undergraduate degrees are clear aids into getting a specific graduate job or, at the very least, to completing a Masters, and it is fine to write about this as a motive.

We are not just talking about Law, Medicine, Engineering, Accounting, Dentistry, Veterinary Medicine, and other "professions". Nursing, Social Work, Primary Teaching, and many more career paths either demand certain degrees, or give credit for having studied a certain degree by reducing the study required for career-specific qualifications later on.

EXAMPLES OF OPENING PARAGRAPHS

****PLAGIARISM ALERT****

Below are examples of how to express each of the reasons above in an opening paragraph. In each instance, I provide two alternatives. This is to give you a feel of how to play around with language and use a variety of vocabulary to express the same thought in different ways. Once you move onto the writing stage, build on these examples to express your personal reason.

Example 1 (reasons 1 and 2):

"I want to spend three years at university studying a subject I love - Business. Whether it be analysing a Balance Sheet or understanding P&L in detail, using psychology in marketing or having a clear strategic vision in a changing marketplace, I enjoy the theory and practice of structured decision-making."

Or:

"To succeed in the challenges a university degree presents, it is important to be motivated and fascinated by the subject matter. Having studied Business at AS and A2 and having looked in detail at the modules and options available (including [XYZ]) I am confident that I will love the three years at your institution."

Example 2 (reasons 1 and 2):

"I want to find out more about several aspects of Business that I have come across during my A-level studies and my own independent activities. The many different ways a Balance Sheet can be constructed and interpreted is one such example, and the modules you offer over the full three years of the degree would give me this level of in-depth understanding."

Or:

"Having the time to explore how business theory and businesses function, work on practical case studies, and talk to leading international experts represents an exhilarating academic opportunity."

Example 3 (reason 3):

"My father runs a small construction business, and seeing the way he has dealt with problems since the start of the Global Financial Crisis has driven my interest in Economics and Management."

Or:

"Hearing my mother, a manager in the NHS, talk about budget planning, staff retention and technological changes has married well with my Economics A-level. It is one thing to consider the theory of marginal costs and quite another to hear about the real human costs of decision-making."

Example 4 (reason 3):

"A school trip to the City of London, and in particular the London Metal Exchange, brought alive the real world power of economics and how decisions made by political or business leaders impact on the lives of millions. It is to gain a better understanding of the connections between these different forces and how the consequences come about that I want to study this subject."

Or:

"My father's employer (Unilever) offered a parent/child work shadowing day in my GCSE year. This insight into the world of business, and especially how to build a brand, gain market share, and keep consumers interested, was the trigger for me choosing Business Studies at A-level and now, after rigorous research, for deciding on Business with Marketing as my degree."

Example 5 (reason 4):

"My high scores in Maths and Further Maths, Physics and Economics, and my medals in Maths and Physics Olympiads, show that I am good at quantitative subjects. I enter the Olympiads because they provide a fun opportunity to apply my knowledge in a different, more creative way. This combination of ability and enjoyment has made my choice of degree easy."

Or:

"I have worked hard at maths from a young age, and, while I may not have reached the 10,000 hours required for excellence (as Gladwell writes in "Outliers"), I am proud of achieving two gold medals and one silver medal in Maths and Physics Olympiads. I want to apply this skill to the quantitative study of economics and economic theory at university level."

Example 6 (reason 5):

"My ambition is to pursue a career in finance. I am yet to decide on the specific path within this field, but I am sure that, whichever direction I choose, this degree, combining detailed quantitative analysis, research, and pragmatic case studies, will be something I enjoy and will give me a great foundation in the skills required."

Or:

"My predicted grades and results so far make me eligible for many excellent universities. I am applying to yours because of the work placements built into the degree, as I think practical experience combined with academic theory is what employers are looking for. I am choosing to do this degree to have better job prospects and because of a genuine academic interest."

Chapter 5

Personal Statement Paragraph 2: SUBJECT-SPECIFIC FURTHER READING

The aim in paragraph 2 is to reference and discuss the relevant books you have read, beyond what you must read for A-level. Simply listing everything you have read is not good enough. You must set out to prove your interest in and aptitude for your chosen course.

To do this, you need to intelligently analyse the ideas you have read about and draw out examples to make specific points. This requires actually reading sections of the books; not necessarily from cover to cover (reading "Introductions" and "Conclusions" plus a couple of relevant chapters goes a long way), but it will take you some time.

Below is a list of relevant books for your subject. For each, I have provided specific ideas and arguments which you could draw out of the texts and weave into your Personal Statement using the quotes I give and your own words. Again, I provide multiple examples for each idea. Use these examples to help you formulate your own ideas using a wide range of vocabulary.

If you are just getting started with extracurricular reading, pick two titles from the list below and go get them from the library or a local bookshop. Start reading immediately. If you have already started reading, the below will give you ideas for other books to read and show you how to work your thoughts into your statement.

Remember the quality of the examples you use is far more important than the quantity of books you have read.

****PLAGIARISM ALERT****

BOOK 1: "Good Strategy / Bad Strategy" by Richard Rumfelt

Idea 1: Identifying what strategy actually is compared to the way it is perceived / presented today, and providing an example of how you have used real strategy in your own decision-making

Quote from book:

"Executives who complain about 'execution' problems have usually confused strategy with goal setting ... Strategy is about HOW an organisation will move forward."

Example:

"I have started developing the skills and understanding I will need for this degree course in my own time, as the material at school does not cover these topics in enough depth, if at all. Initially, my "strategy" was to go to a good university and then get a place on a graduate management programme. Reading Rumfelt's "Good Strategy / Bad Strategy" I realised I had "confused strategy with goal setting". I have now focused on a real strategy - this is the "how" of moving forward, through better study skills, wider reading, and subject-based extracurricular activities."

Or:

"Watching business-based TED talks, taking part in the "Shares for Schools" competition, and entering the Royal Economic Society essay competition are part of my strategy to achieve my goal of getting into a good university. Learning the difference between "goals" and "strategy" came from reading Rumfelt's "Good Strategy / Bad Strategy", much of which will serve me well at university and in my planned career in business management."

<u>Idea 2: Applying your resources and energy to the area where you will get the greatest gain</u>

Quote from book:

"The most basic idea of strategy is ... strength applied to the most promising opportunity."

Example:

"This is my twelfth and final version of my Personal Statement. Rumfelt highlighted in "Good Strategy / Bad Strategy" that effective strategy involves "strength applied to the most promising opportunity". Beyond this Personal Statement, the areas I can control and apply energy to in maximising my university entry chances include ..."

Or:

"I have read many books outside of school to give me a better grounding in the material I can expect at university and to help me understand the exact balance of Economics, Business, Finance, Accounting, and Management I want in my degree. Rumfelt's "Good Strategy / Bad Strategy" confirmed this as a valid strategy in that I have "applied strength to the most promising opportunity." This book built on ideas previously seen in ..."

Idea 3: Learning to be reflective

Quote from book:

"... possibly the most useful shift in viewpoint: thinking about your own thinking."

Example:

"The financial markets and business world are constantly evolving, and static thinking will leave a person or organisation behind. I have already benefitted from advice in Rumfelt's "Good Strategy / Bad Strategy" in which he outlines, in "Thinking Like a Strategist", that it is vital to "...think about your own thinking". I have become a much more reflective learner, looking at what works in my studies and what needs changing or improving: i.e. Rumfelt's "logical and empirical tests". It is this psychology of business management that attracts me to this degree."

Or:

"I want a good job: one that is interesting, offers ongoing opportunities, and pays well enough for me to look after my parents who have given me the chance to be the first in our family to attend university. I needed a strategy to help me get there so I read Rumfelt's "Good Strategy / Bad Strategy" and Dixit and Nalebuff's "Thinking Strategically". The former's ideas on "thinking about your own thinking" helped me become much more methodical (making lists) and empirical (checking what works in my study technique). Through both, I have a better understanding of what makes a good manager, and I look forward to learning more about this at university."

BOOK 2: "Thinking Strategically" by Avinash K. Dixit and Barry J. Nalebuff

<u>Idea 1: Application of a successful strategy in different contexts</u>

Quote from book:

"... if you have the lead the surest way to stay ahead is 'monkey see, monkey do'"

Example:

"My career goal is to work for a financial institution, and this degree is designed to help me get there. Since some of the modules deal with strategy, I read "Thinking Strategically" by Dixit and Nalebuff. The "monkey see, monkey do" strategy (maintaining a lead by copying your followers) is something I have noted amongst financial forecasters."

Or:

"I think the similarity of financial forecasters' predictions can be partially explained by the "monkey see, monkey do" strategy outlined by Dixit and Nalebuff in "Thinking Strategically", a book I read to gain a greater understanding of topics I will encounter in this degree."

Idea 2: Predicting moves (sequential versus simultaneous)

Quote from book:

"Anticipate where your initial decisions will ultimately lead, and use this information to calculate your best choice."

(NOTE: You could compare this text with Covey's "Begin with the end in mind" - the second habit in the "7 Habits of Highly Effective People".)

Example:

"The works of Covey and of Dixit and Nalebuff advocate a clear goal-driven strategy. My goal is to be the first in my family to attend university. To make sure I get there, and for fun, I have been reading books like these, which cover topics underpinning the Business and Management degree."

Or:

"A clear vision and a strategy of implementation is a prerequisite to business success, as highlighted by Covey's "7 Habits", and Dixit and Nabeluff's "Thinking Strategically". Applying this to myself, I used open days, online forums, and university prospectuses to research this course, and, on seeing the emphasis placed on strategy, have started broadening my understanding of it in my free time."

<u>Idea 3: How to create random patterns when needed, e.g. for zero-sum games</u>

Quote from book:

"... a classic mistake in strategic thinking is to believe you can predict your rival's moves simply by wearing his shoes."

Example:

"I thoroughly enjoy taking the lessons learnt from my wider reading on statistics and applying them in the real world. The ideas of how to generate randomness in a zero-sum game, as illustrated in "Thinking Strategically" by Dixit and Nalebuff, have helped me beat several friends (much to their surprise) in tennis competitions, rather than making my usual mistake of "… predict(ing) your rival's moves by wearing his shoes"."

Or:

"The application of min/max strategy in zero-sum games (as I learned in "Thinking Strategically" by Dixit and Nalebuff) and how mathematics and economics can be successfully combined to give solutions in so many practical fields, from sport to warfare, is a direction in which I want to develop my academic career."

(NOTE: It would be interesting to compare this book with Michael Porter's "Competitive Strategy".)

BOOK 3: "The Bottom Billion" by Paul Collier

<u>Idea 1: The economic consequences of "bad governance in a small country"</u>

Quote from book:

"In the bottom billion average life expectancy is fifty years, whereas in the other developing countries it is sixty seven years. Infant mortality (...) is 14% (...). The proportion of children with symptoms of long term malnutrition is 36% (...) as against 20% for other developing countries."

Example:

“Statistics such as those used by Collier in “The Bottom Billion" (50 years life expectancy versus 67 in other developing countries) and his analysis of the "Four Traps” showed me how an understanding of the underlying causes of socioeconomic issues is the first step to change and improve the lives of many.”

Or:

“Comparing the ideas of Collier (“The Bottom Billion”) and Sachs (“Dead Aid”) reinforced how even top economists disagree on the causes of poverty and the limitations of economic development. Whether the very poorest countries are facing one of the “Four Traps”, such as “bad governance in a small country” or being malaria ridden, or not, it is research and analysis that shows the way forward and helps define new strategies to break out of economic and political vicious circles.”

Idea 2: Conflict and war and their role in poverty

Quote from book:

"Civil war is much more likely to break out in low-income countries: halve the starting income of the country and you double the risk of civil war."

Example:

"The close ties between economic policy and social unrest are clearly presented by Collier in "The Bottom Billion", and, most starkly, with the data that halving a country's income doubles its chances of civil war, which in turn reduces income and then living standards. Understanding these connections, and the risks and opportunities they provide to business, is one of the reasons why I want to study this degree."

Or:

"Deciding which country to invest in or where to open a new power plant are vital questions for multinational businesses. Risks, such as the potential for conflict or civil war, need to be taken into account. I gained some understanding of this and other influential factors through reading Collier's "The Bottom Billion"."

Idea 3: "The Natural Resources Trap"

Quote from book:

"... indeed, the surplus from natural resource exports significantly reduces growth"

Example:

"It is hard to understand how many resource-rich countries have such sustained levels of poverty. The successful examples, such as Norway with its Sovereign Wealth Fund or Saudi Arabia and Kuwait as "rentier" states, only serve to highlight the failures in places such as Equatorial Guinea, Nigeria, Sudan, or even Venezuela. Understanding why, as Collier states, "the surplus from natural resource exports significantly reduces growth", is my area of great interest."

Or:

"Norway buys half of Regent Street from the proceeds of its oil-fuelled Sovereign Wealth Fund, but thousands die in the equally oil-rich Niger Delta. The "Natural Resources Trap", as Collier calls it in "The Bottom Billion", is both complex and evolving. Having considered governance and conflict issues, I believe a well-ordered, long-sighted strategy in resource-rich countries is key to alleviating poverty and introducing a potentially virtuous circle of trade. I hope to increase my understanding of these issues in modules [XYZ] offered in your degree."

(NOTE: Compare Collier's ideas with the works of Jeffrey Sachs or Joseph Stiglitz.)

BOOK 4: "End This Depression Now!" by Paul Krugman

Idea 1: The ideas of Keynes and the Great Depression of the 1930s have been forgotten or ignored.

Quote from book:

"The boom, not the slump, is the time for austerity."

Example:

"My generation is experiencing (as Keynes puts it) the "chronic condition of subnormal activity" that is a depression. The waste and suffering of 50% youth unemployment makes no sense if it can be avoided. A deep-rooted interest in tackling this, and in understanding the choices that needed and still need to be made by economists and governments, directed my choice of degree. Krugman quotes Keynes dictum, "The boom, not the slump, is the time for austerity". An in-depth understanding of this technical side of economic and business decision-making is what I want to gain from my degree."

Or:

“Governments appear to have very short memories, often appearing to believe “it’s different this time”. Krugman, quoting Keynes, reiterates, “The boom not the slump is the time for austerity”. On joining the single currency, countries such as Greece did not use the new cheap money wisely. Similarly, neither have many emerging markets with hot money in search of yield, or with natural resource money which has arrived in recent years.”

Idea 2: The euro zone crisis

Quote from book:

“... a common currency, ... efficiency gains ... business costs decline. On the other side there is a loss of flexibility, which can be a big problem if there are large ‘asymmetric shocks’ like the collapse of a housing boom in some but not all countries.”

Example:

“Within Finance I am interested in the management of public debt, particularly in the euro zone. While I closely follow the views of Draghi and Lagarde, it was Krugman’s analysis of “asymmetric shocks” to a single currency system in "End this Depression Now!" which taught me the most. I believe that the need for structural reform is clear, and was pleased when the February 2014 meeting of the G20 finance ministers put this forward in their closing communique. Understanding "what" needs to be done is one matter, but I now want to learn much more about the options on "how", which is why I am pursuing this degree."

Or:

"Attracted to international business both as a degree and career, I keep a close eye on trends and developments in major markets, such as the euro zone. I do my best to understand the theory which underpins events. Krugman's analysis and suggested remedies of the euro zone crisis in "End this Depression Now!" chime most with my thoughts on how governments can deal with the difficulties of "asymmetric shocks"."

BOOK 5: "Nudge" by Richard H. Thaler and Cass R. Sunstein

Idea 1: That there is an "architecture" of choice, and that people's decisions can be influenced (for better or worse) by the way in which that choice is presented.

Quote from book:

"... small and apparently insignificant details can have significant impacts on people's behaviour. A good rule of thumb is to assume that 'everything' matters."

Example:

“Behavioural economics is fundamental to business and society, and I have started exploring it in my own time. How businesses and politicians can “nudge” consumers into specific decisions through “choice architecture” has echoes of the (banned) subliminal advertising of the 1960s. The success of governmental “nudge” actions on smoking are, I believe, now likely to lead to the targeting of sugar.”

Or:

“I find Thaler’s ideas of “libertarian paternalism” and “choice architecture” little different to the centralised macroeconomic controls of China, even if the latter is a significantly heavier “nudge”. Placing carrots at eye level in my school canteen may seem innocent but does raise the question of where this type of control leads.”

<u>Idea 2: That humans are unaware of how biased they are in their decision-making and ignorant of how much they are missing.</u>

Quote from book:

“Although rules of thumb can be very helpful, their use can also lead to systematic biases.”

Example:

"I successfully used the ideas of "systematic bias" in Thaler's "Nudge" when negotiating materials prices for my Young Enterprise team and raising funds for our school charity day."

Or:

"Combining "choice architecture" and "systematic bias", as outlined by Thaler in "Nudge", allowed me to raise more than any other student for our school charity. By raising the donation options well above the accepted norms, people paid more than the average contribution from the previous year, even when contributing less than the smallest amount indicated."

Idea 3: "Dynamic inconsistency", e.g. the fact that people change their mind about doing something they know would be good for them.

Quote from book:

"... self control problems can be illuminated by thinking about an individual as containing two semi-autonomous selves, a far-sighted 'Planner' and a myopic 'Doer'."

Example:

"Understanding how people make financial choices is just one of the appeals of this degree. I read Thaler's "Nudge" to gain a preliminary understanding of how neuroeconomics impacts on this. His ideas were so convincing that I applied them to myself to improve my planning and action for homework and exam preparation."

Or:

"The ongoing battle between an individual's "Planner" and "Doer", as described by Thaler in "Nudge", exemplifies the real world applications of this subject. It is the pragmatic, career-focused approach in this course which attracts me, as opposed to some of the more theoretical options I have seen doing my research on universities."

BOOK 6: "The Signal and the Noise" by Nate Silver

Idea 1: How to predict effectively

Quote from book:

"Prediction is important because it connects subjective and objective reality."

Example:

"I am good at Mathematics, and want to learn how to use ideas such as Bayes's Theorem to predict economic events and guide policy decision-making. The stock market crashes of 2008, 1997, and 1987 should have been easier to predict given the growth in Big Data and computing power, but were not. Silver's "The Signal and the Noise" helped me understand why."

Or:

"Wanting to understand more about Bayesian Theory and its importance in econometrics and prediction, I read Silver's "The Signal and the Noise". The book gave me a clearer understanding of the Global Financial Crisis and a taste of the work I can expect at university level."

<u>Idea 2: To win, your predictions do not need to be the best, just better than the competition.</u>

Quote from book:

"You need to care about accuracy - about getting at the objective truth - rather than making the most pleasing or convenient prediction."

Example:

"I enjoy poker and currently head the school league. The psychology and strategy in poker are interesting, but it is the application of probability in a real world environment which fascinates me. In "The Signal and the Noise" Silver reinforces the difficulty of making clear judgements while embracing uncertainty, "You need to care about accuracy". Reading this highlighted the transferable skills from my interests to business and a Business degree."

Or:

"My interests are probability and strategy. Having read Silver's "The Signal and the Noise" and Dixit and Nalebuff's "Thinking Strategically", I applied ideas from both texts to poker and chess tournaments. As the former says, "You need to care ... about getting at the objective truth". Studying the statistics and methods of both games, as I currently do as a hobby, in a more formal way at university will help me develop as a person and improve my career prospects."

BOOK 7: "Thinking, Fast and Slow" by Daniel Kahneman

Idea 1: People are irrational when faced with financial risk.

Quote from book:

"The four problems (*thought experiments*) highlight the weakness of Bernoulli's model ... the missing variable is the *reference* point"

Example:

"It is the combination of creativity and mathematical reasoning, as demonstrated by Kahneman's "Prospect Theory" in his book

"Thinking, Fast and Slow", that makes me confident I am a good fit for this degree. Taking Maths, Further Maths, and winning gold in the Maths Olympiad demonstrate my mathematical ability, and setting up and profitably running my own online business for two years show my creativity. Learning more about people's natural yet unrecognised bias, and other aspects of behavioural economics and business management psychology, will hopefully lead to my own greater entrepreneurial success in the future."

Or:

"Understanding people's innate risk aversion through "simple" thought experiments and overturning centuries of accepted wisdom (Bernoulli's Utility Theory), as Kahneman did with "Prospect Theory" in "Thinking, Fast and Slow", shows how economics is constantly evolving. Applying this preliminary understanding of behavioural economics and the psychology of business management gained from this book has helped me improve the profitability of my own online business."

Idea 2: "Duration weighting"

Quote from book:

"The time people spend dwelling on a memorable moment should be included in its duration, adding to its weight. A moment can also gain importance by altering the experience of subsequent moments."

Example:

"Reading Kahneman's "Thinking, Fast and Slow", especially his conclusion that, "The time people spend dwelling on a memorable moment should be included in its duration, adding to its weight. A moment can also gain importance by altering the experience of subsequent moments," made me reflect on how much better value the London Olympics may be than I first considered it."

Or:

"How can government spending be considered to be, or to have been, value for money, if the weighting of the imputed values is not correct. In "Thinking, Fast and Slow" Kahneman concludes, "The time people spend dwelling on a memorable moment should be included in its duration, adding to its weight." Reading this, I realised how much greater the cost of Britain's involvement in recent wars must be than is "accounted" for."

BOOK 8: "23 Things They Don't Tell You About Capitalism" by Ha-Joon Chang

Idea 1: Political influence over economics, e.g. protectionism

Quote from book:

"... the living standards of the huge majority of people in rich countries critically depend on the most draconian control over their labour markets - immigration control."

Example:

"In "23 Things They Don't Tell You About Capitalism" Ha-Joon Chang cites the "draconian control" by rich countries to regulate their labour markets. This is easily evidenced by the efforts each spring and summer made by Italy, Malta, and other southern European countries to stem the flow of vessels of refugees (economic and political) from North Africa. The supporters of a "free market" would prefer not to have their nationals undercut in the job market, even if logic says it would promote competition and efficiency."

Or:

"The rise in support for far right political parties in Europe, from Greece, Spain, and France, to the UK and the Netherlands, is partly the result of economic agitprop and of making immigrants the scapegoat for weak economic performance. As Ha-Joon Chang points out in "23 Things They Don't Tell You About Capitalism", "the living standards of the huge majority of people in rich countries critically depend on the most draconian control over their labour markets - immigration control." The major political parties across the developed world are hardening their lines on immigration. I see this as leading to closer economic alliances among those economies outside the "club", which could well outdo the existing dominant world powers this century. A BREXIT may be the way forward."

Idea 2: How countries can become richer

Quote from book:

"Contrary to what is commonly believed the performance of developing countries in the period of state-led development was superior to what they achieved during the subsequent period of market-oriented reform."

Example:

"From my reading and extracurricular activities, I believe that the dominance of free market economics is over and that "new" paradigms are being created. "New" often means revisiting discarded ideas, such as those of Kindleberger or Minsky, or looking with fresh eyes at past successes. As Ha-Joon Chang states in "23 Things They Don't Tell You About Capitalism", "the performance of developing countries in the period of state-led development was superior to what they achieved during the subsequent period of market-oriented reform."

Or:

"As a child brought up with the Internet and the new, technologically-driven ideas of e-commerce and social media-driven politics, I believe that we are at a pivot point. In "23 Things They Don't Tell You About Capitalism" Ha-Joon Chang says, "state-led development was superior to what they (developing countries) achieved during the subsequent period of market-oriented reform." The decisions governments make about how e-commerce and the infrastructure supporting it develop is giving emerging markets the opportunity to leapfrog those developed countries who are slow on the uptake."

(NOTE: Compare with Collier's "Four Traps".)

<u>Idea 3: The multidisciplinary and pragmatic nature of Economics and Business</u>

Quote from book:

"Economists were in fact conspicuous by their absence in the governments of the East Asian miracle economies. Japanese economic bureaucrats were mostly lawyers by training. In Taiwan most key economic officials were engineers or scientists ... as is the case in China today."

Example:

"I am interested in many topics, hence an addiction to TED talks, current affairs blogs, and a range of magazines from Prospect to Nature. While it is Business and Finance I want to study, I was reassured when reading Ha-Joon Chang's "23 Things They Don't Tell You About Capitalism" that the economic and business leaders of the "miracle" economies (Japan, Taiwan, Korea, China) were mainly lawyers, engineers, or scientists. It is the multidisciplinary scope your degree offers to explore my interests and the different facets of business that attracts me."

Or:

"As Ha-Joon Chang states in "23 Things They Don't Tell You About Capitalism", "In Taiwan most key economic officials were engineers or scientists ... as is the case in China today." It is the interdisciplinary aspect of this degree that I find fits best with my future aspirations. I want to know how to channel my imagination and common sense, and know about psychology and strategy, as well as understanding key ratios on a balance sheet."

Chapter 6

Personal Statement Paragraph 3: SUBJECT-SPECIFIC EXTRACURRICULAR ACTIVITIES

Reading books on your subject will gain you a lot of points with admissions tutors, but second place definitely goes to doing some sort of activity outside of school related to your subject. The options are many: watching / attending lectures; regularly reading (and that means not just subscribing to!) a relevant magazine; or joining a society at school - to name just a few. Your involvement in one or more such activities is what you will write about in paragraph 3.

Much of what you can do, watch, or read is available online, which means access to London is not required. As you will see from my suggestions below, just going to a lecture and stating this is not enough. It is vital that you work in your thoughts and reactions to your activities, and detail how they link to your other reading.

The list of activities you could be doing to further your subject knowledge is long. Again, quality is more important than quantity. If you are just starting out, pick three or four different lectures / activities, complete them, and then bring these into your statement. That is plenty.

If you are already involved in one or more of the below, the examples will show you how to link your current activities with your other thoughts on your subject and provide ideas for further activities if you have the time.

****PLAGIARISM ALERT****

1. FREE LECTURES: London School of Economics / University of Oxford

Websites:

(a) LSE: http://www.lse.ac.uk/newsAndMedia/videoAndAudio/channels/publicLecturesAndEvents/Home.aspx
(b) Oxford University: http://www.ox.ac.uk/visitors_friends/whats_on/ and http://podcasts.ox.ac.uk/

Example:

"I have attended several public lectures at the London School of Economics, including "Depression Economics" and "Japan's Lost Decade". Linking these lectures to the responses of Abe and Bernanke to the Global Financial Crisis has given me a taste of the type of thinking and analysis that this degree requires."

Or:

"Lectures on "Depression Economics" and "Japan's Lost Decade" at the London School of Economics public lecture series have helped explain various governments' responses to the Global Financial

Crisis. I have come to the view that quantitative easing was politically rather than economically driven. While it appears to have had an initial positive impact in the US, it is still too early to fully judge; the raising of the debt ceiling in February 2014 was a sign of the ongoing difficulties attached. It is exactly this type of subject matter that excites me about economics at university level."

2. FREE / TICKETED LECTURES: Chatham House (also known as The Royal Institute for International Affairs)

Chatham House (The Royal Institute of International Affairs) is an independent, international affairs think-tank and membership organisation. It is one of the best international research institutions in the world. Noteworthy speakers and attendees fly in from around the globe to take part. Membership is expensive but an investment worth making if you can afford it. A few videos and podcasts are available to download for free on their website, and it is possible to attend some lectures without being a member for a small fee.

Website:

http://www.chathamhouse.org/

Example:

"Globalisation with its interconnectedness has had both positive and serious negative outcomes. This is my opinion after attending a lecture at Chatham House, where speakers included [X] and [Y]. My previous positive view was altered by ..."

Or:

"Attending a lecture at Chatham House, involving [X] and [Y] as speakers, turned my view on globalisation from positive to negative. The tipping point was ..."

3. LECTURES: RSA and Intelligence Squared

The RSA holds multiple lectures on "hot topics". Intelligence Squared is expensive to attend and, by comparison, less intellectual, but is still worth a look for any talks directly relevant to your specific area of interest. Many of the talks from both organisations are archived online and can be watched for free.

Websites:

(a) RSA: http://www.thersa.org/
(b) Intelligence Squared: http://www.intelligencesquared.com/

Example:

"My motivation for attending a Spring Series Intelligence Squared event was to hear [XYZ] talk about her book on food security. I asked a question regarding GM food crops and the ownership of seeds which I had considered when reading the speaker's book."

Or:

"My reflections on [XYZ]'s book [ABC] prompted me to ask her about seed ownership with relation to GM crops in person at an Intelligence Squared event.

4. ONLINE LECTURES: TED Talks / iTunesU / US university websites

Without a doubt, these three are the greatest resource on the web for Personal Statement material. With thousands of topics under specific headings discussed by world leaders in their subject, the videos are usually only 15 - 20 minutes long. As with other lectures, the trick is not to describe what you watched but to engage with the ideas, to give an opinion, and to link these to other extracurricular or school material.

Websites:

(a) TED talks: https://www.ted.com/talks
(b) iTunesU: http://www.apple.com/education/ipad/itunes-u/
(c) US universities: Harvard, Stamford, Yale, Berkley, Columbia

Example:

"With the majority of the world now living in cities we are facing critical choices regarding the allocation of resources. The TED talk

"Four Myths of Urbanisation" highlighted how ghettoes add value and are to be celebrated or, at the very least, permitted."

Or:

"Watching the TED talk "Four Myths of Urbanisation" reinforced the complexity of economic choices by overturning my preconceptions about globalisation and giving me a different understanding of its positive impact - something I want to gain more of from this degree."

5. LECTURES: Royal Economic Society (RES)

Most Business or Finance candidates will write that they read the Economist, far fewer will write that they listen to or attend lectures at the RES. If you are not in London, listen to them online. The articles and areas for discussion are well worth mentioning in your Personal Statement.

Website:

http://www.res.org.uk/view/webcasts.html

Example:

"By seeking out relevant articles and lectures, I have been actively following the debate on the business and financial consequences of independence for Scotland. The recent Royal Economic Society debate on the pros and cons showed how broad a view an economist must have, one which encompasses obvious issues, such as national debt and currency union, as well as complex, international issues, such as the potential difficulty of direct EU participation."

Or:

"Wanting to study Business and Accounting, I found the recent Royal Economic Society debate on Scottish independence illuminating. In highlighting issues such as untangling bilateral trade agreements and establishing financial procedures for settling tax payments (health, pension, unemployment) made by Scottish citizens, it helped me see how important the application of practical, financial mathematics is in finding potential solutions - one of the reasons why this degree so interests me."

6. LECTURES: Royal Geographical Society (RGS)

Most prospective Economics, Management, and Business students talk about the importance of globalisation and the power of emerging markets. Few students, however, take advantage of the Royal Geographical Society's rich resource of online lectures and articles, which cover topics highly relevant to these subjects.

RGS lectures are both streamed and archived online. You will find lectures on the impact of globalisation, inequality, global warming (or not), and other physical changes (e.g. the opening of the Arctic sea routes as relevant for Korea and Russia) which will rapidly alter the way business is done, decide what is produced where, and affect how it is transported.

(NOTE: make sure you know your BRIC / N 11 / MIST / FRAGILE FIVE countries.)

Website:

http://www.rgs.org/HomePage.htm

Example:

"As an economist, and hopefully future employee of a large global firm, I am especially interested in the emergence of Sub-Saharan Africa as an economic force. Listening online to a recent Royal Geographical Society talk on infrastructure developments in that region expanded my understanding of the challenges I read about in Collier's "The Bottom Billion"."

Or:

"The modules a degree in [XYZ] offers on African economic growth is a major reason for my application. My family's East African heritage has prompted my strong interest in developments in this region, and my long term goal is to work for a firm with activities there. Having read Collier's "Four Traps" in "The Bottom Billion", it was exciting to hear about how these are being overcome in a streamed Royal Geographical Society lecture on how the new railroad infrastructure cooperation will alter Rwanda's landlocked difficulties."

7. ACTIVITY: Model UN

If you do not already have a Model UN at school, get the support of a teacher to organise one. By taking part in this you will be up to speed with many major global influences and concepts. Participating in meetings and discussing hot topics while representing a specific country or department develops your thinking, creativity, and teamwork skills in a way much appreciated at university.

Website:

http://www.unausa.org/

Example:

"At the Model UN meeting held in Geneva, I represented the Republic of South Africa in a debate on energy. I spoke as the country's Energy Minister, and considered the consequences of energy shortage on industrial production."

Or:

"Taking part in the Model UN in Geneva and speaking as Energy Minister for the Republic of South Africa built on my understanding of current energy issues (fracking / liquified natural gas) gained from the Economist and various TED talks."

8. ACTIVITY: Model European Parliament

Europe will remain a significant trading partner and a major influence on our economy, whatever course European politics takes in the coming months. The benefits of participating in the Model European Parliament, such as improving your knowledge of global political and economic affairs, and honing your thinking and presenting skills, are similar to those of participating in the Model UN.

Website:

https://www.mepnederland.nl/

Example:

"I took part in the Model European Parliament 2014 to develop my understanding of how politics and economic matters work together to influence businesses. I was the first person from my school ever to become involved, and wrote a report on how I think it helped me develop my research, decision-making, and problem-solving skills."

Or:

"Believing it is important for students to understand about the wider influences on business and trade, I took the initiative of organising our school's participation in the Model European Parliament for the first time, and generated support amongst a group of students and two teachers to make it happen."

9. ACTIVITY: School Societies

Joining or starting a society related to your chosen subject is one of the initiatives I recommend most during Personal Statement workshops and Sixth Form Route-Mapping sessions. This shows all the usual competencies (teamwork, independent research, time management) and can easily give you three lines of content for your Personal Statement. Whether the society organises meetings weekly, fortnightly, or each term, what matters is the wide range of activities that can be talked about in your statement.

Suggested activities for your school society (to name just a few of the options):

(a) Individual members research a topic of special interest and give a 15-minute presentation to their peers.
(b) As a group the society watches a chosen TED talk or other lecture, and then discusses it.
(c) Prominent / successful local people involved in the subject area are invited in to speak.

(d) As a group the society enters competitions.
(e) The society publishes a blog or, once a term, a short newspaper.
(f) The group reads a book or article before the meeting and discusses their thoughts.

Example:

"Reading Collier's "The Bottom Billion" while preparing a post on poverty alleviation in Sub-Saharan Africa for the school's Economics Society blog (which I set up with teacher support last year) emphasised how important steady investment in infrastructure is for economic growth."

Or:

"The TED talk on climate change we watched in the school's Business Society tied in with many of the ideas I had learned about in a Royal Geographical Society lecture on [XYZ], and underlined how important it is for multinational corporations to take ongoing geographical changes into account."

10. ACTIVITY: Debate Chamber

Attending a Debate Chamber course (£425 for five days) will widen and deepen your understanding of your subject area. It is particularly useful if you are applying to a university which may interview you. The experience will provide you with at least two or three lines of content for your statement, and is often a springboard for additional further reading and thus more Personal Statement content.

Typical courses include: http://www.debatechamber.com/summerschools/economics-summer-school/

Website:

http://www.debatechamber.com/

Example:

"Discussing the economics of happiness at a Debate Chamber weekend was thought-provoking and assured me that a Business and Management degree is a good fit for my skills and interests. Understanding what motivates and, as importantly, what does not motivate people is key to personal and business success. I built on this experience by reading Covey's "7 Habits Of Highly Effective People"."

Or:

"The ideas I considered at a Debate Chamber weekend inspired me to read Covey's "7 Habits Of Highly Effective People". Hearing about "happiness economics" made me look at how I worked and how I could be more efficient. It is Covey's type of analysis that I want to do at university level in a Business and Management degree, namely learning how to identify what works."

11. ACTIVITY: Bright Network

This fantastic organisation (yes, I do speak at their annual "Bright Festival") is a great way for prospective bankers, lawyers, and computer scientists to get ahead of the career curve. By taking part in their events, you show that you are thinking about your career before most other students, which by extension says a lot about your motivation to study at university.

Website:

https://www.brightnetwork.co.uk/

Example:

"As I am already considering my career direction - banking - I applied, and was accepted (after a CV check and telephone interview) out of thousands of applicants, to attend Bright Network's Investment Banking Conference. Talking to many representatives from the finance sector confirmed that an Economics degree with a strong quantitative element would provide an excellent foundation for my future aspirations."

Or:

"Talking to representatives of financial giants, such as HSBC, Citigroup, and UBS, at Bright Network's Investment Banking Conference confirmed that a quantitative Economics degree will give me the right tools (such as [XYZ]) for this career path. Conference attendance was selective, dependent on a test of both my written and spoken skills (including a 15-minute telephone interview).

12. ACTIVITY: Pure Potential

I used to work with this organisation so can tell you that their events provide you with excellent information about university applications, financing yourself through university, and ways to get your career started early. Involvement in Pure Potential shows your willingness to see whether or not a specific university is right for you. As part of a small group you are given a Pure Potential Ambassador, who is a current student at the university where the event is being held and who can give you inside information on university life. As with open days and taster days, putting this in your Personal Statement shows that you are making a considered choice for your life post Sixth Form.

Website:

http://www.purepotential.org/

Example:

"I have chosen this degree and this university, despite the costs, as I believe that in the long run it will develop me as a person and make me more employable. Attending a Pure Potential event day confirmed that, even though there is no tradition in my family of attending university, it is both a viable and sensible choice."

Or:

"Researching in detail my next academic step has involved the HEAPS Guide, open days, taster days, and a Pure Potential event. The latter assured me that the cost is an investment in my future, and, as such, I am committed to achieving the best result in a subject I love.

13: ACTIVITY: Insight Days at Investment Banks

Some major investment banks offer insight days and even summer internships for Sixth Form students. These are highly competitive because once you are on their books it is much easier to get preferential selection for internships at that bank a year later as a university student. This can then lead to a full time job offer. Being "fast-tracked" as a result of making an application and getting on a scheme in Sixth Form means you may avoid the ever more stressful form filling, interview process, and assessment centre days required from most undergraduates. In other words, if you want to be a banker, this is the best way in.

To get on these programmes, you need to have a good CV and write answers to questions on motivation and competency such as:

(a)) Why investment banking? (100 words)

(b) Why this bank - what differentiates us? (100 words)
(c) Tell us about a time when you have effectively communicated within a team to overcome a challenge. (150 words - please give details of context, action you took, and results achieved.)
(d) What motivates you? (100 words)
(e) Tell us about a time when you had a strict deadline (not academic related) and needed to prioritise work to get a result. (150 words - please give details of context, action you took, and results achieved.)

Banks offering such programmes include:

Goldman Sachs (girls only): http://www.goldmansachs.com/careers/why-goldman-sachs/diversity/diversity-emea.html
JP Morgan: http://careers.jpmorgan.com/student/jpmorgan/careers/europe/schools/insightday
Morgan Stanley: http://www.morganstanley.com/about/careers/eprograms.html
Credit Suisse (Steps to Success Internship Programme): https://www.credit-suisse.com/uk/en/careers/campus-recruiting/our-business/internship-programs-emea/diversity-programs.html
Nomura: http://www.nomura.com/europe/careers/insight_programs/index.shtml

Example:

"Forward planning is something I consider important. While not having confirmed that I want a career in banking, I have applied for and have been accepted on the Credit Suisse Steps to Success

Internship Programme. This will allow me to see how financial markets operate in a practical rather than purely theoretical way, and give me early information on career choices."

Or:

"One of the main career routes from this degree (as shown by your careers page) is banking and finance. To find out whether or not I have the right character to fit in this industry sector, I applied for and was accepted on a Goldman Sachs women-only insight programme. Being accepted was the result of my grades, a CV check, a 500 word motivational letter, and a telephone interview. I believe it is worth the effort, as it will serve as a head-start in career planning that leaves more time for study at university."

14. ACTIVITY: University Taster Days

These subject-specific university experience days are fantastic proof that you are serious about choosing the right course for you. Why? Places on these days disappear very quickly and the fact that you applied early enough to get a place shows forethought, research skills, and time management.

Website:

Check out the offerings from the specific universities / university departments you are interested in.

Example:

"Early application successfully got me on the UCL Business and Finance Taster Day. The day confirmed that I had made the right decision to take Additional Maths and that I will easily deal with the quantitative aspects of the course. Talking to current students gave me a clear idea of how to budget, especially when living in halls, and the importance of getting actively involved in university societies."

Or:

"Extensive research prior to my application, including, among other activities, the UCL Taster Day for Business and Finance, makes me confident that this university course is right for me."

15. ACTIVITY: Shadowing at Cambridge and UNIQ (Oxford University Summer Schools for State School Students)

As with taster days, summer schools, and open days, getting on the Cambridge Shadowing Scheme shows commitment to finding out about university life. As you can imagine, it is highly competitive but Cambridge University is genuinely looking for high potential candidates from a wide variety of backgrounds. The scheme involves a two-day stay in Cambridge spending time with a current undergraduate studying the subject you are interested in. The whole trip is funded by the university, including accommodation, food, and travel costs (in most cases).

Attending a summer school (usually a week) gives you an insight into university life, an understanding of the type of work that higher level study entails, and concrete ideas on what the admissions tutors are looking for when you apply. Run by Oxford University, UNIQ is one of the most competitive summer schools out there. To apply, you will need to submit a mini Personal Statement about your motivation. All of the hints and tips for your UCAS Personal Statement apply equally when writing this. For one-on-one support with writing this, please contact me via my website (www.gwynday.com).

Websites:

Cambridge: http://www.applytocambridge.com/shadowing/
Oxford: http://www.uniq.ox.ac.uk/

Example:

"Being accepted on the University of Cambridge shadowing scheme has confirmed that a challenging course at a leading university is right for me. Sitting in on lectures gave me a real understanding of the difference in standard between A-level and degree-level study. I left very motivated to find out more about my subject, and confident that the independent study and dedication required at university play to my strengths."

Or:

"As the first person in my family to attend university, I was apprehensive before attending the week-long Oxford University UNIQ summer school. During my time there, I was fascinated by the breadth of subject matter on offer in Economics (including my particular area of interest - emergent African economies) and excited by the variety of student life. I am now certain that studying at university is the best step for me."

16. COMPETITIONS: Royal Economic Society and Marshall Society Essay Competitions

Taking part in essay competitions (even if you do not win) shows you in a good light several ways. You had the initiative to find out that the competitions existed and then act on that information. You completed independent research without (or with only minimal) support from school, which is what will be expected of you at university. To complete the trio, you did all of this on top of your current studies, which shows you can prioritise and deal with pressure.

Websites:

(a) RES (deadline June 30th 2014): http://www.res.org.uk/view/essayEduTraining.html
(b) Marshall Society: http://marshallsociety.com/index.php

Example:

"I chose to do my Royal Economic Society essay entry on the economic consequences of the global growth of fracking in the oil industry. I considered which countries would benefit short term (USA) and longer term (China), and looked at the potential environmental damage (especially water depletion) in terms of negative externalities."

Or:

"The trade off between positive and negative externalities due to the growth in global fracking showed me the difficulty of imputing values for a cost benefit analysis. Whether the regeneration of US heavy industry outweighs the depletion and reduction in quality of water reserves is something I need university-level thinking tools to judge."

17. MEDIA: Coverage of the Third Plenum

When applying for economics or business-based subjects, China cannot be ignored. There are daily updates, weekly articles, and a plethora of lectures online, but you can go one step further and look at the macro picture as outlined at the Third Plenum in November 2013. As the name suggests, this is the third meeting of China's Central Committee at which, traditionally, new political and economic directions are decided or old ones reinforced. In 2013 the announcements focused on: further raising living standards of the rural poor; continuing to expand infrastructure; working towards easing pollution; relaxing the one-child policy; and accelerating RMB influence. The consequences of all of these decisions are already being felt around the world.

Direct records are not available online but plenty of news outlets provide detailed summaries.

(a) BBC: http://www.bbc.co.uk/news/world-asia-china-24910434
(b) Guardian: http://www.theguardian.com/world/2013/nov/15/china-one-child-policy-relaxed-reforms
(c) Forbes: http://www.forbes.com/sites/junhli/2013/11/24/highs-and-lows-from-chinas-third-plenum/
(d) Business Insider: http://www.businessinsider.com/7-china-experts-on-third-plenum-2013-11

Example:

"Business in the twenty-first century basically means China. To gain a deeper understanding of Chinese goals and strategy I followed reports on the 2013 Third Plenum. The decisions around internal growth and the shift away from being purely export-driven has caused much of the volatility we have seen in 2014."

Or:

"I believe that the RMB is going to overtake the USD as the world's reserve currency and, as such, will make it a vital area to study at university. Your department's links with China and the modules you offer will help me build on the ideas I have already gained from following media reports on the Third Plenum, PBOC transparency initiatives, and the challenge posed by the US-driven Trans-Pacific Partnership."

18. MEDIA: DAVOS / World Economic Forum

This week-long conference, which takes place in late January / early February, is a "must know" for anyone genuinely interested in Economics or Business. You get more billionaires gathered in one spot than at any other time or place during the year. Supposedly, people go to attend presentations and lectures. In reality, the heavy lifting gets done during the informal networking and it is for this that the world's powerful, rich, and infamous come. Some say that more global strategy is decided here than at the UN.

The theme this year (2014) was inequality, which the world's most important business people and politicians have finally realised is a big threat to global stability. The themes coming out of the conference change year by year, so your Personal Statement needs to specifically reference the theme and/or presentations given.

Website:

http://www.weforum.org/

Example:

"I enjoy the broader aspects of Business and the way it can shape society. My introduction to behavioural economics came via reading Thaler's "Nudge". I think similar ideas to those used to reduce smoking in the UK could be used to promote entrepreneurialism and reduce social inequality, which is a pressing issue internationally, particularly given its focus at Davos this year."

Or:

"The focus this year at Davos' World Economic Forum on growing social inequality prompted me to consider the ways that behavioural economics (as I read about in Thaler's "Nudge") might help address this."

19. MEDIA (online): IG Index

Various "spread betting" companies allow you to "paper trade" (i.e. fake money) the financial markets, and there are multiple fantasy trading website competitions. Showing an understanding of companies and other asset classes, such as forex, bonds, or commodities, and the factors that drive their prices can work well depending on the specific modules your chosen course offers. To get to grips with the concepts related to trading see my website for more details (www.gwynday.com).

Website:

http://www.ig.com/uk

Example:

"To gain a better understanding of how companies work and to see if I could successfully identify undervalued companies, I have been paper trading on a fantasy investment league. Over a six-month period my return on investment (ROI) is 29%. I have been considering companies in the weeks before their annual reports and seeking to judge when the market is underestimating performance. I believe such research will help me in the demands of this Accounting and Finance degree."

Or:

"Tracking macroeconomic indicators and investing based on them has given me a better picture of the way business, economics, and politics influence each other. Betting that Abenomics would weaken the Yen; the Australian Central Bank would drive down the Aussie; and that tapering would hit the Indonesian Rupiah has made money (on my father's account). I want to further my understanding through the macroeconomic modules this degree offers."

20: ACTIVITY: Playing Poker, Backgammon, Chess, or Bridge

If you say you are interested in game theory, strategy, statistics, or probability, it makes sense for you to become involved in one of the above. Universities are looking to see that you have a genuine interest in your subject and in what that subject entails. Whether it is friendly play in a school club or at regional / national / international level, the fact that you choose to get involved in your own time means you are both developing skills and have a genuine enthusiasm for something that can be directly related to your course.

Websites:

www.cardplayer.com
www.pokerology.com

Example:

"This Accounting degree involves several modules on risk and risk analysis. As both a poker and backgammon player, I am used to making quick calculations on probability and weighing the results in terms of a specific strategy. I am ranked top in our school Poker League and regularly play, and win, against adults at backgammon."

Or:

"Two years ago I was thirtieth out of thirty in the school's Poker League. Reaching the top of that league has taught me much about weighing risk and judging probability. Along with understanding the numbers, Accounting is about the people who work with those numbers and the strategies they employ. poker and backgammon have developed my skills in making the right decisions and learning from my mistakes when I get it wrong."

OTHER RELEVANT ACTIVITIES

21. University Open Days

The end of the summer term is the best time to attend these, not the autumn when you are under pressure from the increased workload of A2 (or equivalent). When talking about your time at open days in your Personal Statement, be sure to say you went with a mission to understand what the course would be like and detail how the trip confirmed or reinforced your conviction to apply to university.

22. Self-study a Language

Starting early with an unusual foreign language is attractive to both universities and employers, mostly because it shows independent study and initiative-taking. For you personally, having a second language gives you access to a wider social group when you get to university.

Thinking long term, economics and business are global. At the end of your degree your objective (usually) is to get employed. Most businesses value languages not just because it can be useful when talking to clients, but equally because knowledge of a language shows a different way of thinking, flexibility of mindset, and empathy.

Potential languages to learn include:

(a) Portuguese - Portugal, Brazil, and several emerging African countries, such as Angola and Mozambique.
(b) Bahasa Malay - Malaysia, Indonesia (200 million speakers), and other South-East Asian countries.
(c) Russian - one of the most important countries / economies in the world.

If you already speak a language in addition to English because of your family background, you can emphasise how you have focused on developing economic and business vocabulary through wider reading of magazines and books in the target language, as well as listening to business news broadcasts and discussions in that language online or on satellite TV.

23. EPQ (Extended Project Qualification)

If your school offered this, I hope you decided to take it. This can easily be worth six lines or even a full paragraph of a Personal Statement. Given that the qualification involves considerable reading and the determination to complete a 4,000 word essay to university standard in your own time, it clearly indicates the calibre of person you are. What is important about the EPQ is that you can choose any topic and this allows you to explore, compare, and contrast ideas on an area of Economics or Business which really interests you and to form your own opinion. When it comes to your Personal Statement, you should mention the relevant EPQ-related books, lectures, and even interviews you may have arranged.

Website:

http://www.aqa.org.uk/programmes/aqa-baccalaureate/extended-project/the-aqa-epq

24. Young Enterprise and Target 2.0

These two are the least impressive subject-specific extracurricular activities - unless you become at least regional finalists. Pretty much every Business, Finance, and Economics candidate will take part, and then say how important their role was in the team and how they learnt about teamwork, decision-making, marketing, pricing, etc. If everybody says it, then there is nothing to make you stand out. Simple.

25. Prizes

Prizes - whether at school, regional, national, or international level - show that you are prepared to compete. Universities want students to be driving for a First in their degree studies and will be impressed that you are willing to be tested voluntarily and to put yourself under pressure.

26. Maths / Physics / Chemistry Olympiads

If your degree contains any quantitative element - which for subjects such as Economics, Business, and Finance is highly likely - it is worth taking part in the Maths / Physics / Chemistry Olympiads or the UK Maths Challenge (held annually). If you do not do well, then no need to mention it. If you get a medal or award, this again shows you have the requisite skills to deal with a quantitative degree.

Websites:

British Maths Olympiad: http://www.ukmt.org.uk/individual-competitions/british-mathematical-olympiad/
British Physics Olympiad: http://www.physics.ox.ac.uk/olympiad/index.html
British Chemistry Olympiad: http://www.rsc.org/Education/events-and-competitions/Olympiad/About.asp
UK Maths Challenge: http://www.ukmt.org.uk/individual-competitions/

27. UBS Outstanding Students Award

Leading investment bank UBS has teamed up with Pure Potential (see 12 above) to recognise and celebrate the achievements of the brightest state-school Sixth Former in the country. This is a great credit to have on your Personal Statement because it shows your aptitude, initiative, and motivation.

Website:

http://www.purepotential.org/events/ubs-award

28. Peer Subject Coach / Private Tutor

Universities know that the best way to understand a subject is to teach it. If you can break a topic or concept down and successfully explain it to others, then you will surely understand it yourself. Knowing how to do that will make it easier for you to grasp new concepts at university. From an entrepreneurial perspective, running your own tutoring business gives you a superb understanding of the business theory you will look at in your degree.

29. Subject Ambassador

This is another area I strongly encourage in the schools I visit. If this does not exist in your school or Sixth Form College, get it set up. Being a subject ambassador means giving talks to both parents and students (individually and together) to promote your subject and convince them of the benefits of studying it at GCSE or A-level (or equivalent). Universities will definitely appreciate that you enjoy the subject so much that you are prepared to promote it. The soft skills you develop doing so are an added bonus.

30. Listening to Radio 4

Programmes such as “Money Box”, “Wake Up To Money”, and “In Our Time”, along with many others, provide very different viewpoints on current and historical matters linked to your subject. Few Sixth Formers listen to these and mentioning them will make you stand out.

Website:

http://www.bbc.co.uk/radio4

Chapter 7

Personal Statement Paragraph 4: NON SUBJECT-SPECIFIC ACTIVITIES

In paragraph 4 you will write about the non subject-related activities you are involved in. This may sound easy compared to other sections in the statement, but actually requires just as much careful thought.

The tendency, here, is for students to write a long shopping list of activities, eager to demonstrate how busy and active they are. This is not good enough. Far more interesting to admissions tutors is to see that you have done one or two activities for an extended period of time, and taken them to a high level of achievement. Again, the "what" is not that important, but the "how" you have shown commitment and improvement over several years is.

You may have your own examples already. If you do not, choose two or three from the list below which are relevant to you. For each activity, work out the skills you developed and how these skills will help you at university and/or in your chosen course. This information is what you need to write down.

****PLAGIARISM ALERT****

1. Sport

Example:

"As a break from my studies I play cricket and would like to play for the university team. Playing for the school and the county has instilled self-discipline. I know that if I do not turn up to practice or to a match because I am tired or have homework, I will be letting others down, and, consequently, I have learnt to organise my studies effectively."

Or:

"Over the past four years I have taken my enjoyment of cricket from being a "knock-around" with friends to playing for my county team in national competitions. I have learnt to organise my studies effectively to maintain my grades and still attend training and matches for my school and county teams. I want to contribute to my university cricket team, though my academic work, as it does now, will always come first."

2. Music

Example:

"Achieving Grade 8 on the violin represents five years of commitment and progress. Preparing for and playing in concerts has helped my attention to detail and focus, as I need to be constantly aware of what is happening and adapt to unexpected changes. Performing solos (the largest audience was 300) has built confidence in my ability to achieve what I set out to do."

Or:

"Performing a violin solo in front of 300 people was the culmination of reaching Grade 8 and five years hard work. I fully commit to whatever I start, and this same sense of achievement is what I expect when I graduate."

3. Drama

Example:

"One of the scariest things I ever did was three years ago, when I agreed to appear in a school play. I did it as I knew I needed to improve my confidence at speaking in public. Acting has given me that confidence and so much more. Since then, I have joined a local drama group and passed several LAMDA exams. I am now even happy to sing on stage. Thinking and working towards a project involving so many others, most of whom do not appear on stage, has given me a real understanding of teamwork, and prepares me well for the third-year group project in this degree."

Or:

"Playing Othello in a youth amateur dramatics society in front of 150 people showed me that I had conquered my fears of speaking in public. Three years ago I heard through family friends that most degrees require project work and formal presentations. I hated public speaking but was determined to be the first in my family to attend university, so I volunteered for the school play and, from there, took LAMDA exams and joined other theatre projects. I am at the point where I enjoy acting but, more importantly, the experience has taught me that if I rise to the challenge I can successfully achieve my goals."

4. Duke of Edinburgh's Award

Example:

"Getting my Silver Duke of Edinburgh's Award, and particularly completing the expedition, was a significant achievement for me, both because I am from an inner city school and rarely spend time in the countryside and because I suffer from asthma. My team helped me a lot, and I learned the value of supporting others to achieve their best. From research, I have seen that this course involves project work, often with diverse groups, and I think the DofE experience will greatly help with this."

Or:

"Aside from academics, my greatest achievement at school has been completing all three Duke of Edinburgh's Awards. The Expedition for my Gold Award was in the Black Mountains in Wales. The weather turned against us badly and one of the team had asthma attacks. As a learning experience of decision-making under pressure and the importance of getting group consensus, I think it will be a major help in my future."

5. Part-time job

Example:

"For the last two years I have worked part-time as a waitress in my local pub and will continue full-time over my AS and A2 summer holidays. I am saving what I earn because I want to enjoy myself at university, try new activities, and graduate with as little debt as possible. Being responsible for ten tables with sometimes up to 40 customers means good organisation, diplomacy when things go wrong, and willpower to keep going."

Or:

"Dealing with sometimes angry customers, taking responsibility for cashing up hundreds or thousands of pounds, and training new staff have been aspects of my waitressing job for the last two years. I took the job as I want to be as financially independent as possible and graduate from university with lower debt than most. Considered by my employers as highly efficient and reliable, I have been offered full-time work in the pub whenever I want, an offer which I will take up this (AS) summer and next."

6. Self-employment

Example:

"A year ago I started my own business buying and selling items I think teenagers want - from iPhone covers to t-shirts. I negotiate with suppliers I find online and then market the products through my social media network. Juggling my time and dealing with the many small problems which occur have shown me how important attention to detail and thinking ahead are in business."

Or:

"I currently run two small businesses in my spare time. Firstly, I taught myself how to repair cracked screens on iPads and iPhones. I needed some specialist equipment, for which I borrowed a small sum from my parents (already repaid), and then started marketing online. Secondly, I teach IT skills to the over fifties. My focus is Excel, though clients often buy extra lessons to learn other skills which interest them. I have made and saved £8,000 in the last two years, even after self-funding two inter-rail holidays to explore southern and eastern Europe."

7. CCF (Combined Cadet Forces)

Example:

"While not considering a career in the Armed Forces, I joined the CCF for the personal development opportunities it offers. Now leading a platoon, I understand a lot more about what it takes to organise others and how that is only possible if I am efficient and detail-oriented myself."

Or:

"I feel I am ready for the demands of university and much of that is due to my involvement in the CCF. The self-discipline required, whether looking after equipment or during drills and exercises, has instilled in me a strong work ethic. I have learnt to organise my time efficiently and get tasks done before rather than on the deadline. Since becoming Platoon Leader I have greatly improved my communication, leadership, and decision-making skills, most notably when dealing with and motivating younger cadets. Knowing how to achieve my goals will help me get a good degree."

8. Community involvement

Example:

"My religion (Hinduism) is important to me. As an active member in our local Temple, I help organise both ceremonies and charity events, including a food bank service where people, unable to buy enough food for themselves, can eat for free. Whether washing dishes, cleaning floors, or doing something more complicated, I get a great deal of satisfaction from this work, and will be looking for wider pro-bono activities at university."

Or:

"As a member of the Jewish faith, I take great pleasure in giving back to a community which gives me so much. The two activities I divide my attention between are working with the elderly infirm and helping mentally handicapped children. In both cases I have learnt patience, especially in finding different ways of communicating. Most importantly, I know how wrong it is to prejudge people and how there is something to learn from everyone - an attitude which I will apply in university life."

9. Political involvement

Example:

"For the last year I have been involved with the Muslim Youth Council of Great Britain. I attend meetings which discuss issues both within the Muslim community and concerning links with the wider world. I am especially proud of a presentation I gave on how to encourage more Muslims to cycle to work and college rather than taking public transport or driving. At university I want to help promote diversity, and would love to become an ambassador reaching out to prospective applicants."

Or:

"I am and will continue to be politically active. I believe in diversity but since the end of Aim Higher funding and the introduction of higher university fees, I have seen a drop in the number of young Muslims in my community applying to university. Through involvement in the Muslim Youth Council of Great Britain I have spoken at several community events in my borough to raise aspiration and promote further education."

10. Charity work / volunteering

Example:

"I started volunteering at my local Cancer Research shop after several relatives were diagnosed with this illness. I am impressed by the dedication that goes into the research for a cure and the care given by organisations to people with this condition. I only work four hours a week but feel all contributions make a difference. After speaking to customers with cancer, I trained for and completed a half marathon, raising £300 which I donated to my local shop."

Or:

"On my university open day visits I made a particular effort to speak with students who do charity work, as it is important to me to continue the support I have given for the last two years. I am proud to have completed a half marathon and raised £300 for Cancer Research UK (CRUK), as previously I had never run more than 800 metres at school. Having several relatives who have undergone treatment for cancer makes it very personal, and this is one of the reasons why I volunteer for four hours weekly at the CRUK shop on my local high street."

11. Other hobbies

Example:

"In my spare time I play traditional Indian musical instruments, such as the sita. I give performances locally, both individually and as part of a group. While being open and international in outlook (I want to be involved in the Erasmus Programme at university), I believe it is important to have a connection with my culture's traditions. Since starting five years ago, I have now achieved proficiency and continue to practise every day."

Or:

"I build rockets as my hobby. I enjoy the research and problem-solving involved in getting the rocket to go higher or further each time without increasing the size, and am part of an online community which exchanges ideas and tips. Going to rocket fairs I have made friends nationally and internationally. Thinking about how to continuously improve and refine my work is a skill which will transfer well to university."

12. Travel

Example:

"Travelling internationally with my family, school, and independently has opened my eyes to how lucky we are in the UK. While citizens do have real problems, they are minor when compared to what faces so many others globally. My family originally comes from Nigeria. Trips there and to neighbouring countries have motivated me to push myself academically and use the resources available to me. I know there are millions of children who would love to have access to the education I have, but are prevented by circumstance."

Or:

"Coming to Britain three years ago from Kazakhstan has involved overcoming major language and cultural obstacles. I think the perspective I have gained from knowing two completely different worlds has made me more flexible and understanding in my approach to others."

13. Prefect / school positions

Example:

"Being appointed a Prefect has given me my first taste of organising, managing, and motivating others. One of my duties is speaking in assembly and at some parent events. This has built my sense of responsibility and made me confident about speaking in front of others."

Or:

"I am proud of my involvement in the school's Charity Committee, where I am the Treasurer and report directly to the School Bursar. Part of our work involves organising approximately six events each year. Last year we donated over £5,000 to two schools in Uganda, with whom we are twinned. As Treasurer I keep the accounts and arrange the distribution of funds for equipment required at events. One of my biggest jobs is chasing people for paperwork and accurate numbers."

14. Head Boy / Head Girl

Example:

"Being elected Head Girl by my peers and the Senior Leadership Team required a review of my achievements and contributions, and several public speeches to explain to the school body what I thought

I could bring to the role. I direct a team of ten prefects and we are included in consultations regarding changes which impact Years 12 and 13. I have given several speeches to parents of existing and potential students. This combination of leadership, teamwork, and getting things done should help me successfully contribute to university life."

Or:

"I believe I was elected as Head Boy for two main reasons. Firstly, I get on with a wide range of students, including rugby team mates, choir friends, and Economics and Debating Society peers. Secondly, I get things done and am not afraid to lobby and approach senior staff if the situation requires it: e.g. in Year 11 I initiated links between our school debating society and an underperforming school in our area."

Chapter 8

Personal Statement Paragraph 5: WRAPPING UP

The final paragraph of your Personal Statement is the easiest. In it, you need to cover two of the four suggested points below. Aim for between two and four lines in length - short and sweet is definitely best.

You can:

1. Summarise what you have already said to demonstrate you are a good fit for the course and the university.

2. Refer to some of the specific skills that your first choice universities have said you will gain or develop during the degree.

3. Mention specific types of career path outlined on university websites as being possible following this degree.

4. Talk about your interest in furthering your studies to Masters level.

****PLAGIARISM ALERT****

Example 1 (demonstrating points 1 and 4):

"Through wider reading, lectures, and summer schools I believe I have shown my genuine interest in the subject beyond just school studies. I aim to go on to Masters level after my undergraduate degree and am prepared to work hard to achieve my goal."

Or:

"My goal is to achieve a First class undergraduate degree and then complete a Masters in the area of most interest to me; which could, indeed, be something I have not yet studied. I hope I have shown my interest to be deeply rooted and to go beyond just school level."

Example 2 (demonstrating points 2 and 3):

"I am highly motivated by the opportunity to learn about [insert aspect of the course] and then apply this in one of the wide range of career directions outlined as options following this degree. I look forward to attending careers events and company visits during my studies. Thank you."

Or:

"This degree and the financial management skills I will acquire is my first step towards a successful career. The events and company links you have, which I heard about on open days, encompassing investment banks and financial advisory firms, underline that this is the right degree choice for me."

Example 3 (demonstrating points 2 and 3):

"Enhancing my research, computing, project teamwork, and quantitative analysis skills through this degree will provide me with an excellent foundation for whichever career direction I pursue. The extra support provided by the Careers Service, including courses and internship / job application advice, is an added bonus."

Or:

"I am looking forward to making the most of the extra courses and internship / job application support offered by the Careers Department. The idea of applying in my future career the research, computing, project teamwork, and quantitative analysis skills I will gain during this degree is a motivating long-term prospect."

Chapter 9

REFINING YOUR PERSONAL STATEMENT TO MAKE IT UNIQUE

By this point you will have the basic content of your Personal Statement mapped out. Now you must refine it and make it more personal. This chapter will help you.

The steps below aim not to add in further information on books you have read or accolades you have collected; instead, they show you how to improve the language and tweak the structure to leverage the work you have already done, and ultimately make your Personal Statement unique to you.

Follow each step carefully, and allow yourself time to experiment with structure and various turns of phrase.

****PLAGIARISM ALERT****

Step 1: Take your almost finished draft and split it into sections. Label each section to establish exactly what it adds to your statement and what it proves about you as an applicant to admissions tutors. See the example and the labels in *italics* below.

Example Draft Personal Statement

Paragraph 1 / Reason for choosing course

[There are specific areas of your subject you want to specialise in, which are offered by that course.]
I want to find out more about several aspects of Business that I have come across during my A-level studies and my own independent activities. The many different ways a balance sheet can be constructed and interpreted is one such example, and the modules you offer over the full three years of the degree would give me this level of in-depth understanding.

Paragraph 2 / Evidence of interest in and aptitude for subject, using further reading and lectures

[Evidence 1: Further reading]
While I closely follow the views of Draghi and Lagarde, it was Krugman's analysis of "asymmetric shocks" to a single currency system in "End this Depression Now!" which taught me the most.

[Evidence 2: Lectures]
I have attended several public lectures at the London School of Economics, including "Depression Economics" and "Japan's Lost Decade". Linking these lectures to the responses of Abe and Bernanke to the Global Financial Crisis has given me a taste of the thinking and analysis that this degree requires.

[Evidence 3: Reading newspapers and self-study of language]
Studying two European languages (German and Spanish) at A-level, in addition to Maths and Economics, I have taught myself enough economic vocabulary to read the financial pages of newspapers in those countries, including a recent article in the Handelsblatt about how the yields (Renditen) on bonds are influenced by geopolitics and shifting exchange rates (Wechselkursen).

[Evidence 4: Own opinions based on further reading]
Along with following current affairs, this degree will require the imagination to see how a changing political and global economic landscape will influence policy choices. Tracking Switzerland's immigration referendum and Turkey's shift towards Russia has convinced me of the likelihood of major structural reforms within the euro zone.

[Evidence 5: Research into offering at that specific university]
My interest in Finance is the management of public debt with particular reference to the euro zone. Your university's close ties with European counterparts, the Erasmus Programme, and modules on public finance are major draws.

[Evidence 6: Own opinions based on further reading]
I am interested in the complex, ethical dilemmas involved in Finance, whether this be public finance decision makers deciding which part of a nation's budget to cut when this will have a direct impact on the quality of life of the poorest, the approval of accounts by prestigious auditing firms and credit rating agencies of

companies such as Enron and RBS, or the creation of low tax pathways for firms such as Starbucks and Google.

Paragraph 3 / Further evidence of interest and aptitude, using subject-specific extracurricular activities

[Evidence 1: Skills developed through extracurricular activities]
I chose my A-levels to give me a strong quantitative background and use my extracurricular activities to develop softer skills.

[Evidence 2: Student politics - interest in broader current affairs]
Becoming involved in my school's Student Council and then joining the youth section of the Labour Party, I am currently active in preparations for the European Elections and early stage constituency policy discussions regarding the party's manifesto for the general election.

[Evidence 3: Student Council - taking initiative and seeing things through to successful completion]
Through the Student Council I have successfully introduced two initiatives. Firstly, we now have recycling bins for each different type of waste in every building (previously, we only had two). Secondly, I proposed turning a large flower bed into a vegetable garden so that students can understand properly about planting and growing food. We donate any produce to a local food bank charity.

Paragraph 4 / Other extracurricular, unrelated to subject but evidencing qualities useful for university

[Evidence 1: Sport - relevant skills for university]
As captain of the school netball team and a member of the county squad, I have become adept at decision-making and analysis, both individually and as part of a group, which I hope will help with the challenges involved in this degree.

[Evidence 2: showing determination and confidence]
As a female in mostly male classes I sometimes need to push to make myself heard, which I think I have done well.

[Evidence 3: Music - commitment and capacity for hard work]
Performing violin solos in front of 300 people was the culmination of reaching Grade 8 and five years hard work. I fully commit to whatever I start and the same sense of achievement is what I expect when I graduate.

<u>Paragraph 5 / Wrap up</u>

[Evidence 1: Skills to be learned at university, and career opportunities post university]
Enhancing my research, computing, teamwork, and quantitative analysis skills, I am confident this degree will provide me with an excellent foundation for whichever career direction I pursue. The extra support provided by the Careers Service, including courses and internship / job application advice, is an added bonus.

Step 2: Move around the sections to give your Personal Statement the shape you want.

Reworked Example 1:

Studying two European languages (German and Spanish) at A-level, in addition to Maths and Economics, I have taught myself enough economic vocabulary to read the financial pages of newspapers in those countries, including a recent article in the Handelsblatt about how the yields (Renditen) on bonds are influenced by geopolitics and shifting exchange rates (Wechselkursen). I have attended several public lectures at the London School of Economics, including “Depression Economics” and “Japan's Lost Decade”. Linking these lectures to the responses of Abe and Bernanke to the Global Financial Crisis has given me a taste of the thinking and analysis that this degree requires.

My interest in Finance is the management of public debt with particular reference to the euro zone. Your university's close ties with European counterparts, the Erasmus Programme, and modules on public finance are major draws. While I closely follow the views of Draghi and Lagarde, it was Krugman's analysis of “asymmetric shocks” to a single currency system in “End this Depression Now!” which taught me the most. I am interested in the complex, ethical dilemmas involved in Finance, whether this be public finance decision makers deciding which part of a nation’s budget to cut when this will have a direct impact on the quality of life of the poorest, the approval of accounts by prestigious auditing firms and credit rating agencies of companies such as Enron and RBS, or the creation of low tax pathways for firms such as Starbucks and Google. Along with following current affairs, this degree will require the imagination to see how a changing political and global economic landscape will influence policy choices. Tracking Switzerland's immigration referendum and Turkey's shift towards Russia has convinced me of the likelihood of major structural reforms within the euro zone. I want to find out more about several aspects of Business that I have come across during my A-level studies and my own independent activities. The many different ways a balance sheet can be constructed and interpreted is one such example, and the modules you offer over the full three years of the degree would give me this level of in-depth understanding.

I chose my A-levels to give me a strong quantitative background and use my extracurricular activities to develop softer skills. Through the Student Council I have successfully introduced two initiatives. Firstly, we now have recycling bins for each different type of waste in every building (previously, we only had two). Secondly, I proposed turning a large flower bed into a vegetable garden so that students can understand properly about planting and growing food. We donate any produce to a local food bank charity. Becoming involved in my school Student Council and then joining the youth section of the Labour Party, I am currently active in preparations for the European Elections and early stage constituency policy discussions regarding the party's manifesto for the general election.

As a female in mostly male classes I sometimes need to push to make myself heard, which I think I have done well. Performing violin solos in front of 300 people was the culmination of reaching Grade 8 and five years hard work. I fully commit to whatever I start and the same sense of achievement is what I expect when I graduate. As captain of the school netball team and a member of the county squad, I have become adept at decision-making and analysis, both individually and as part of a group, which I hope will help with the challenges involved in this degree.

Enhancing my research, computing, teamwork, and quantitative analysis skills, I am confident this degree will provide me with an excellent foundation for whichever career direction I pursue. The extra support provided by the Careers Service, including courses and internship / job application advice, is an added bonus.

Reworked Example 2:

My interest in Finance is the management of public debt with particular reference to the euro zone. Your university's close ties with European counterparts, the Erasmus Programme, and modules on public finance are major draws. While I closely follow the views of Draghi and Lagarde, it was Krugman's analysis of "asymmetric shocks" to a single currency system in "End this Depression Now!" which taught me the most. I have attended several public lectures at the London School of Economics, including "Depression Economics" and "Japan's Lost Decade". Linking these lectures to the responses of Abe and Bernanke to the Global Financial Crisis has given me a taste of the thinking and analysis that this degree requires.

I want to find out more about several aspects of Business that I have come across during my A-level studies and my own independent activities. The many different ways a balance sheet can be constructed and interpreted is one such example, and the modules you offer over the full three years of the degree would give me this level of in-depth understanding. I am interested in the complex, ethical dilemmas involved in Finance, whether this be public finance decision makers deciding which part of a nation's budget to cut when this will have a direct impact on the quality of life of the poorest, the approval of accounts by prestigious auditing firms and credit rating agencies of companies such as Enron and RBS, or the creation of low tax pathways for firms such as Starbucks and Google. Studying two European languages (German and Spanish) at A-level, in addition to Maths and Economics, I have taught myself enough economic vocabulary to read the financial pages of newspapers in those countries, including a recent article in the Handelsblatt about how the yields (Renditen) on bonds are influenced by geopolitics and shifting exchange rates (Wechselkursen). Along with following current affairs, this degree will require the imagination to see how a changing political and global economic landscape will influence policy choices. Tracking Switzerland's immigration referendum and Turkey's shift towards Russia has convinced me of the likelihood of major structural reforms within the euro zone.

I chose my A-levels to give me a strong quantitative background and use my extracurricular activities to develop softer skills. Becoming involved in my school Student Council and then joining the youth section of the Labour Party, I am currently active in preparations for the European Elections and early stage constituency policy discussions regarding the party's manifesto for the general election. Through the Student Council I have successfully introduced two initiatives. Firstly, we now have recycling bins for each different type of waste in every building (previously, we only had two). Secondly, I proposed turning a large flower bed into a vegetable garden so that students can understand properly about planting and growing food. We donate any produce to a local food bank charity.

As captain of the school netball team and a member of the county squad, I have become adept at decision-making and analysis, both individually and as part of a group, which I hope will help with the challenges involved in this degree. As a female in mostly male classes I sometimes need to push to make myself heard, which I think I have done well. Performing violin solos in front of 300 people was the culmination of reaching Grade 8 and five years hard work. I fully commit to whatever I start and the same sense of achievement is what I expect when I graduate.

Enhancing my research, computing, teamwork, and quantitative analysis skills, I am confident this degree will provide me with an excellent foundation for whichever career direction I pursue. The extra support provided by the Careers Service, including courses and internship / job application advice, is an added bonus.

Step 3: Having found a sequence you like, start changing / replacing words to make it uniquely yours. The highlighted words in the example statement can be replaced with the suggested options in the table below. Use this process as a guide on how to refine your own statement.

(NOTE: Though you will still think of your Personal Statement in terms of "blocks" of content, you will not use paragraph indentations or even new lines on the online UCAS form. As mentioned, this is because the 4000 character limit simply does not leave you enough space to do so.)

My interest in Finance is the management of public debt with particular reference to the euro zone. Your university's close ties with European counterparts, the Erasmus Programme, and modules on public finance are major draws. While I closely follow the views of Draghi and Lagarde, it was Krugman's analysis of "asymmetric shocks" to a single currency system in "End this Depression Now!" which taught me the most. I have attended several public lectures at the London School of Economics, including "Depression Economics" and "Japan's Lost Decade". Linking these lectures to the responses of Abe and Bernanke to the Global Financial Crisis has given me a taste of the thinking and analysis that this degree requires.

I want to find out more about several aspects of Business that I have come across during my A-level studies and my own independent activities. The many different ways a balance sheet can be constructed and interpreted is one such example, and the modules you offer over the full three years of the degree would give me this level of in-depth understanding. I am interested in the complex, ethical dilemmas involved in Finance, whether this be public finance decision makers deciding which part of a nation's budget to cut when this will have a direct impact on the quality of life of the poorest, the approval of accounts by prestigious auditing firms and credit rating agencies of companies such as Enron and RBS, or the creation of low tax pathways for firms such as Starbucks and Google. Studying two European languages (German and Spanish) at A-level, in addition to Maths and Economics, I have taught myself enough economic vocabulary to read the financial pages of newspapers in those countries, including a recent article in the Handelsblatt about how the yields (Renditen) on bonds are influenced by geopolitics and shifting exchange rates (Wechselkursen). Along with following current affairs, this degree will require the imagination to see how a changing political and global economic landscape will influence policy choices. Tracking Switzerland's immigration referendum and Turkey's shift towards Russia has convinced me of the likelihood of major structural reforms within the euro zone.

I chose my A-levels to give me a strong quantitative background and use my extracurricular activities to develop softer skills. Becoming involved in my school Student Council and then joining the youth section of the Labour Party, I am currently active in preparations for the European Elections and early stage constituency policy discussions regarding the party's manifesto for the general election. Through the Student Council I have successfully introduced two initiatives. Firstly, we now have recycling bins for each different type of waste in every building (previously, we only had two). Secondly, I proposed turning a large flower bed into a vegetable garden so that students can understand properly about planting and growing food. We donate any produce to a local food bank charity.

As captain of the school netball team and a member of the county squad, I have become adept at decision-making and analysis, both individually and as part of a group, which I hope will help with the challenges involved in this degree. As a female in mostly male classes I sometimes need to push to make myself heard, which I think I have done well. Performing violin solos in front of 300 people was the culmination of reaching Grade 8 and five years hard work. I fully commit to whatever I start and the same sense of achievement is what I expect when I graduate.

Enhancing my research, computing, teamwork, and quantitative analysis skills, I am confident this degree will provide me with an excellent foundation for whichever career direction I pursue. The extra support provided by the Careers Service, including courses and internship / job application advice, is an added bonus.

Other phrasing options and sample vocabulary:

Use the suggested variations below to tweak your Personal Statement and make the language less repetitive and more expressive.

close ties	close links, connections, good relationship, partnership with / between
counterparts	institutions, peers, organisations
closely follow	monitor, track, keep a close eye on, review daily
attended	been to, listened to, taken part in
linking	connecting, bringing this together with, marrying this with, drawing parallels between
has given me a taste	introduced me to, has shown me what to expect, has given me a good idea, was a valuable insight into
I want to find out more	I want to explore further, wanting to go deeper, I want a more complex understanding, I am looking to build on
have come across	have encountered, have explored, have considered, have found interesting
the many different ways	the multiple ways, the range of ways, the different options, the various methods
the modules you offer	the course choices, the study options, the range of subject matter, the breadth of course opportunities
would give me an in-depth understanding	would let me see in detail, would show me at a granular level, would allow me to better understand
studying	learning, taking, choosing, opting for
I have taught myself	independently learning, teaching myself, self-studying, learning in my own time
tracking	keeping up to date with, following the top stories on, enjoying relevant news stories on, monitoring the progress of
convinced	persuaded, turned me, directed me, brought me to the opinion that

likelihood of major structural reforms	strong possibility of (major structural reforms), major chance of significant changes, high probability of serious changes to the structure of
strong quantitative background	to enhance my numerical literacy, to be numerically literate, to have an in-depth understanding of numbers
becoming involved	actively participating, deciding to become involved, wanting to engage with, becoming a member, joining
I have successfully introduced	successfully introducing, initiating, driving, bringing to success / fruition
so students can understand properly	to give students an understanding of, to show students, getting students to see, to help show students that
I have become adept at	I have developed the skill, becoming adept / good at, learning how, developing my skills of
both individually and as part of a group	for myself and others, in various situations, irrespective of how many are involved
I hope will help with the challenges involved in this degree	which I see as supporting my degree, will complement my undergraduate studies, will contribute to the skills needed at undergraduate level
was the culmination of	was the result of, resulted from, was the reward for, came about because of
I fully commit	I wholly commit, committing fully to, giving maximum effort

sense of achievement	feeling of success, satisfaction of achieving, successfully accomplishing
I am confident	I am certain, I am convinced, I believe
excellent foundation	good grounding, prepares me well, is strong preparation
whichever career direction I pursue	for my future career, in the future, for my professional career after university, post university, whichever professional route I take
is an added bonus	just adds to the attraction, makes it even more attractive, motivates me even further, is an additional motivation

Chapter 10:

SIX EXAMPLES OF PERSONAL STATEMENTS

By this stage your Personal Statement will be taking shape. Now spend some time comparing it to the examples of strong Personal Statements below and see if you need to make any further changes.

The example statements are divided into the sections detailed in Chapter 2. This is to show you the thought process behind each one. As mentioned, when you submit your own statement via UCAS, it will not be spaced like this because of the character limit.

In the examples, each section is labelled to show you what is being addressed, what that proves about the student, and how much "space" this idea is given. If your statement is well structured, you will be able to break it down in a similar way.

****PLAGIARISM ALERT****

EXAMPLE 1

Paragraph 1

[Reason for applying: career goal]
My ambition is to pursue a career in finance. Within this field, I am yet to decide on the specific path. Whether investment banking, consultancy, audit, or the finance department of a major firm, I am

sure that whichever direction I choose, this degree, combining quantitative analysis, detailed research, and pragmatic case studies, will be something I enjoy and will give me a great foundation in the skills required.

Paragraph 2

[Further reading linked to the career goal outlined in paragraph 1 and what motivates student academically.]
Statistics such as those used by Collier in "The Bottom Billion" (50 years life expectancy versus 67 in other developing countries) and his analysis of the "Four Traps" showed me how understanding the underlying causes of socioeconomic issues is the first step to change and improve the lives of many. I want to study this degree to gain the basic knowledge and tools to take my interest in economic policy and planning to the next level.

[Further reading linked to own opinions on current economic affairs.]
My interest lies in economic policy in general, rather than just emerging markets. Reading "End This Depression Now!", "The Big Short", and closely following the responses of Bernanke, Abe, Draghi, and Osborne to the Global Financial Crisis (GFC) has convinced me that, whilst quantitative easing is unsustainable, it was an effective and necessary measure to address the GFC. The fact that Greece has so successfully (along with Portugal, Spain, Italy, and Ireland) returned to the bond market, turned the corner regarding property prices, and has a falling debt to GDP ratio underlines this. The ongoing costs of restructuring, namely high

unemployment and a deflating economy, are painful in human terms but a necessary evil, I believe.

Paragraph 3

[Subject-specific extracurricular activity (EPQ) showing research skills and independent study.]
Writing my EPQ on the currency price movements of four countries (Indonesia, Turkey, UK, and Japan) against the USD since 2007 allowed for extensive research on macroeconomics and the market response to economic indicators (e.g. inflation, GDP, CPI, and PMI) and policy shifts. I have learnt to use professional websites (www.seekingalpa.com), regional economic reports by international consultancies (PwC, Deloitte), and to read trend signals on currency charts.

[Subject-specific extracurricular activities (Olympiads and work experience) showing capacity to improve skills, willingness to work hard outside of formal school environment, and ability to organise time effectively.]
Taking part in the UK Maths Challenge and the Maths and Physics Olympiads has sharpened my quantitative skills. These were improved even further by the two-week work experience with a local accounting firm, which I organised independently this summer. I feel I dealt well with the workload and far longer hours than I am used to at school - good preparation for university.

[Subject-specific extracurricular activity (open days and taster days) showing that student has taken university application has seriously.]
I attended three university Open Days this summer and two subject-specific Taster Days, all of which confirmed that I have a good understanding of the intellectual and financial demands this degree will make on me, and the benefits I will gain both in terms of personal development and career prospects.

[Subject-specific extracurricular activity (school society) proving self-motivated interest in subject and capacity for university study.]
At school I am an active member of the Economics Society and gave two talks last year, on "Austerity versus Printing Money" and "How I would invest £10m". I surprised my classmates by not choosing equities and bonds, but rather by going for alternative asset classes, such as stamps, wine, and other collectibles. It is discussions on topics such as these with like-minded students that I look forward to at university. My school is almost totally white, working / lower middle class, and I am keen to hear views of more international and ethnically diverse students. This is why I am applying to universities with especially wide-ranging cohorts as well as a high league table ranking for Economics.

Paragraph 4

[Non subject-specific extracurricular activity (sport) showing long term dedication to excellence and willingness to help others.]

My main hobby is Taekwando which I have practised for ten years. I achieved my black belt last year, and I now help coach lower grade students.

Paragraph 5

[Wrapping up: motivated and ambitious for future.]
I bring focus and commitment to whatever I choose to do, and fully intend to gain a First for my undergraduate degree to give me the widest range of further study or career path options in the future.

EXAMPLE 2

Paragraph 1

[Reason for applying: career aspirations and course opportunities, linking in further reading and specific area of interest.]
I want a good job - one that is interesting, offers ongoing opportunities, and pays well enough that I can look after my parents who have given me the chance to be the first in our family to attend university. I needed a strategy to help me get there so I read Rumfelt's "Good Strategy / Bad Strategy" and Dixit's and Nalebuff's "Thinking Strategically". The former's ideas on "thinking about your own thinking" helped me become much more methodical (list making) and empirical (checking what works in my study technique). I now have a better understanding of what makes a good manager (whether of myself or of others) and look forward to

learning more about management theory in this degree. The specific modules you offer, the opportunity for a dissertation in an area of my choice, your links to industry, and the extensive post-university and job application support you provide, all mean this is the right place for me.

Paragraph 2

[Further reading: linking book to part-time job, showing lateral thinking and broader interest in subject.]
Books by Stephen Covey and Terry Leahy (CEO of Tesco for 20 years) gave me a deeper understanding of myself and how to work with others. My motivation for reading Leahy's book was partly because I have a part-time job in the supermarket, but mostly because I am fascinated by the scale of the operation, the psychology of selling, and the logistics of the supply chain. With so many potential solutions, how do you find the optimum? The firm's American failure alongside their ongoing success in eastern Europe and Asia (Tesco Lotus) underlines the complexity of growing even major firms beyond their home market. The modules you offer on the international nature of business and the fact that I will be regularly doing project work with international students will give me an insight into this.

Paragraph 3

[Subject-specific extracurricular activity (Young Enterprise) proving relevant skills for course and interest in business.]

Taking part in the Young Enterprise competition gave me hands on experience of pricing and of making choices between potential marketing channels. My team reached the regional finals and, though we did not win, I learned a lot about how to improve presentations (useful for this degree) and deal with pressure.

[Subject-specific extracurricular activities (coaching and listening to radio) showing student to be self-motivated, aware of own short-comings, and determined to succeed.]
At school I am a peer coach and run a weekly Maths clinic for younger students. I follow current business news through Radio 4's "Wake Up To Money", which I heard about from my Business Studies teacher. Taken aback by how much I did not know, I have started actively honing my commercial awareness by reading the Economist and business pages of The Telegraph in the school library. I am having more difficulty with the "jargon" in the Financial Times articles but am making progress.

[Subject-specific extracurricular activity (open days and online research) showing that student has taken university application has seriously.]
I have taken choosing which universities to apply to seriously, using subject league tables to profile the best universities in line with both my GCSE profile and my predicted grades (which I think are fair). Visiting two university open days and reading student-written blogs at my target universities has been helpful. Several students from my school have gone on to my two top choices and I spoke to them at a school careers / UCAS day.

Paragraph 4 (bringing in some of paragraph 3)

[Subject-specific extracurricular activity (Model European Parliament) and non subject-specific (future interests for university) showing wider interest in subject and that student enjoys diverse range of activities.]
I am looking forward to developing personally at university; for example, I have noted the many different sports that students can try, and I intend to use some of the money earned from my supermarket job for activities such as parachuting and hang gliding, as they are subsidised. I took part in the Model European Parliament 2014 to develop my understanding of how politics and economic matters work together to influence businesses. I was the first person from my school ever to get involved and have given feedback on how I think it helped me develop skills, such as research, decision-making, and problem-solving.

Paragraph 5

[Wrapping up: strongly motivated]
I believe I have the skills and motivation to do well in this course and take full advantage of university life.

EXAMPLE 3

Paragraph 1

[Reason for applying: find out more about specific area of interest.]
I want to find out more about several aspects of Business that I have come across during my A-level studies and my own independent activities. The many different ways a balance sheet can be constructed and interpreted is one such example, and the modules you offer over the full three years of the degree would give me this level of in-depth understanding.

Paragraph 2

[Further reading: discussing how a book has changed her view.]
My interest in Finance is the management of public debt with particular reference to the euro zone. While I closely follow the views of Draghi and Lagarde, it was Krugman's analysis of "asymmetric shocks" to a single currency system in "End this Depression Now!" which taught me the most.

Paragraph 3

[Subject-specific extracurricular activity (tracking current affairs): showing wider interest and ability to form own opinion.]
I am interested in the complex ethical dilemmas involved in Finance, whether this be public finance decision makers deciding which part of a nation's budget to cut when this will have a direct impact on the quality of life of the poorest, the approval of accounts by prestigious auditing firms and credit rating agencies of companies such as Enron and RBS, or the creation of low tax pathways for firms such as Starbucks and Google. Along with

following current affairs, this degree will require the imagination to see how a changing political and global economic landscape will influence policy choices. Tracking Switzerland's immigration referendum and Turkey's shift towards Russia has convinced me of the likelihood of major structural reforms within the euro zone.

[Subject-specific extracurricular activity (self-study): showing initiative and interest in subject.]
Studying two European languages (German and Spanish) at A-level, in addition to Maths and Economics, I have taught myself enough economic vocabulary to read the financial pages of newspapers in those countries, including a recent article in the Handelsblatt about how the yields (Renditen) on bonds are influenced by geopolitics and shifting exchange rates (Wechselkursen).

[Subject-specific extracurricular activity (lectures): linked to further reading showing lateral thinking, ability to analyse, and research into university offering.]
I have attended several public lectures at the London School of Economics, including "Depression Economics" and "Japan's Lost Decade". Linking these lectures to the responses of Abe and Bernanke to the Global Financial Crisis has given me a taste of the thinking and analysis that this degree requires. Your university's close ties with European counterparts, the Erasmus Programme, and modules on public finance are major draws.

[Subject-specific extracurricular activity (student politics): showing determination, motivation, and other relevant skills for university study.]

I chose my A-levels to give me a strong quantitative background and use my extracurricular activities to develop softer skills. Becoming first involved in the school Student Council and then joining the youth section of the Labour Party, I am currently active in preparations for the European Elections and early stage constituency policy discussions regarding the party's manifesto for the general election. Through the Student Council I have successfully introduced two initiatives. Firstly, we now have recycling bins for each different type of waste in every building (previously, we only had two). Secondly, I proposed turning a large flower bed into a vegetable garden so that students can understand properly about planting and growing food. We donate any produce to a local food bank charity.

Paragraph 4

[Non subject-specific extracurricular activities (music and sport): showing long term dedication to excellence, leadership skills, and ability to work in a team.]
As a female in mostly male classes I sometimes need to push to make myself heard, which I think I have done well. Performing violin solos in front of 300 people was the culmination of reaching Grade 8 and five years hard work. I fully commit to whatever I start and this same sense of achievement is what I expect when I graduate. As captain of the school netball team and a member of the county squad, I have become adept at decision-making and analysis, both individually and as part of a group, which I hope will help with the challenges involved in this degree.

Paragraph 5

[Wrapping up: skills she wants to learn at university and ambitions for the future.]
Enhancing my research, computing, teamwork, and quantitative analysis skills, I am confident that this degree will provide me with an excellent foundation for whichever career direction I pursue. The extra support provided by the Careers Service, including courses and internship / job application advice, is an added bonus.

EXAMPLE 4

Paragraph 1

[Reason for applying: specific area of interest, plus a trigger.]
The work required to get a degree can be challenging, which is why it is important to be motivated and truly enjoy the subject matter. Having already studied Business at AS and A2 and having looked in depth at the modules and options available (including [XYZ]), I am confident that I will love the three years at university. A school trip to the City of London, and in particular the London Metal Exchange, brought alive the real world power of economics and how the decisions made by political or business leaders impact on the lives of millions. To gain a better understanding of the connections between these different forces and how the consequences come about is why I want to study this subject.

Paragraph 2

[Further reading: discussing how it has changed his / her view.]
From my reading and extracurricular activities, I believe that the dominance of free market economics is over and that "new" paradigms are being created. "New" often means revisiting written off ideas such as those of Kindleberger or Minsky, or looking with fresh eyes at past successes. As Ha-Joon Chang states in "23 Things They Don't Tell You About Capitalism", "the performance of developing countries in the period of state-led development was superior to what they achieved during the subsequent period of market-oriented reform." The evolution of Communism into the current hyper-successful Chinese model, with its merging of entrepreneurialism and central control, and the West's (USA's) response to combat the threat, e.g. The Asian Pivot and establishing the TPP, are what makes this subject both fascinating and relevant to me.

<u>Paragraph 3</u>

[Subject-specific extracurricular activity (Icebreakers): showing specific area of interest, self-motivation, and ability to see bigger picture.]
Your university's links in Asia and the opportunity to take part in an exchange programme are highly appealing. Last year I became a member of '<u>Icebreakers</u>' - the youth arm of the 48 Group - which fosters relations between China and UK businesses, and have arranged a six-week summer course in Beijing. I admire the way China has the foresight to "build too big", especially in terms of infrastructure, to allow for economic growing room. This is contrast

to the UK where, with projects such as HS2 and the difficulties around the next airport development of the South East, it feels as if we are always trying to catch up.

[Subject-specific extracurricular activity (Youth Parliament): showing specific area of interest, knowledge of current affairs.]
The opportunity to immerse myself in China will allow for a more detailed understanding of how economic changes, such as the RMB's growing role in trade and the likelihood of it becoming a reserve currency in the mid term, will impact on the rest of the world. Getting involved with the Youth Parliament has made me much more aware of current economic policy towards Asia (Cameron's visits to India and China) and of how even more interconnected British business will be with these regions this century.

[Subject-specific extracurricular activity (running own business): linking hands-on experience with academic theory and showing dedication to going to university.]
My running of a local tutoring service and organising three small sponsorships from local businesses have enabled me to fund this trip. I found managing my tutoring business far more informative than Young Enterprise, experiencing firsthand how different your thinking and motivation are when it is your own money. This applies with regards to my approach to university, in that I see it as an investment in myself and my future.

<u>Paragraph 4</u>

[Non subject-specific extracurricular activities (drama): showing ability to overcome own fears and determination to succeed.] Playing Othello in a youth amateur dramatics society in front of 150 people showed me that I had conquered my fears of speaking in public. Three years ago I heard through family friends that most degrees require project work and formal presentations. I hated public speaking but was determined to be the first in my family to attend university, so I volunteered for the school play and, from there, took LAMDA exams and joined other theatre projects. I am at the point where I enjoy acting but, more importantly, the experience has taught me that if I rise to the challenge I can successfully achieve my goals.

Paragraph 5

[Wrapping up: summary of interest and future academic goal.] Through my wider reading and reflection I believe I have shown my genuine interest in the subject beyond just school studies. I aim to go on to Masters level after my undergraduate degree and am prepared to work hard to make my ambition reality.

EXAMPLE 5

Paragraph 1

[Reason for applying: trigger linked with further reading and specific offering in that course.]

Comparing the ideas of Collier ("The Bottom Billion") and Sachs ("Dead Aid") reinforced how even top economists disagree on the causes of poverty and the limitations of economic development. Whether facing one of the "Four Traps", such as "bad governance in a small country" or being malaria ridden, or not, it is research and analysis that shows the very poorest countries the way forward and helps define new strategies to break out of economic and political vicious circles. The USA's reluctance to give greater power to smaller countries within the framework of the IMF is just one example of the overlap between politics and economics, and the hypocrisy at work. The modules you offer would allow me to explore the macroeconomic in combination with the geopolitical, and even now I am looking forward to the prospect of a dissertation of my choice in the third year.

Paragraph 2

[Further reading: connecting this with current affairs, showing ability to analyse and depth of interest.]
Recent developments in Ukraine show evidence of Collier's ideas. One of the poorest nations in Europe, its dangerous combination of a wealth of shale oil, corrupt government (even if democratically elected), and a combative neighbour resulted in chaos - "Civil war is much more likely to break out in low-income countries: halve the starting income of the country and you double the risk of civil war."

[Further reading and lectures: showing specific area of interest, lateral thinking, and self-motivation.]

I attended a Spring Series Intelligence Squared event because one of the speakers was [XYZ] and I had read her book on food security. I asked a question regarding GM food crops and the ownership of seeds, which I had considered when reading the book.

Paragraph 3

[Subject-specific extracurricular activity (following current affairs): showing ability to put reading into a bigger context.]
It will be fascinating to see the extent to which the disruptive actions in Crimea and the West's sanctions upon Russia impact on global wheat prices, and it is making such connections which excites me about this subject. I particularly want to understand in greater detail the emergence of alternative paradigms and pathways as the world pivots east.

[Subject-specific extracurricular activities (open days and self-studying a language): showing motivation and determination to do well.]
Having checked the resources at three university open days, I know that you offer the opportunity to take a language over the full duration of the course, in addition to my undergraduate degree. I intend to study Russian and have already started independently learning the basic structures and vocabulary using a Rosetta Stone package (which I asked for as my Christmas present).

[Subject-specific extracurricular activities (essay competition): showing willingness to compete and research skills.]

I chose to do my Royal Economic Society essay entry on the economic consequences of the global growth of fracking in the oil industry. Having looked in this essay at which countries would benefit short term (USA) and longer term (China), and the potential environmental damage (especially water depletion) in terms of negative externalities, I now believe that Russia's recent intervention in Ukraine was closely linked to their huge fracking oil reserves (as well as the military base). This intersection of economic choices (Gazprom switching from USD to the euro) and long term strategy (Putin signing a 30 year oil deal with China) is viscerally exciting, and I am committed to learning as much as I can.

Paragraph 4

[Non subject-specific extracurricular activities (CCF and volunteering): providing evidence of leadership and organisational skills.]
While not considering a career in the Armed Forces, I joined the CCF for the personal development opportunities it offers. Now leading a platoon I understand a lot more about what it takes to organise others and how that starts with being efficient and detail-oriented myself. Volunteering at my local Cancer Research shop came about as the result of several relatives being diagnosed with this illness. I am impressed by the dedication that goes into the research for a cure and the care given by such organisations. I only work four hours a week but feel all contributions make a difference. After speaking to customers with cancer I trained for and completed a half marathon, raising £300 to donate to my local shop.

Paragraph 5

[Wrapping up: career ambitions and reiterating good fit for course.]
This degree is my first step towards a successful career. The events and company links you have, which I heard about on open days, encompassing investment banks and financial advisory firms, assure me that this is the right choice.

EXAMPLE 6

Paragraph 1

[Reason for applying: good at the subject, plus evidence to prove it.]
My high scores in Maths and Further Maths, Physics and Economics, and my medals in Maths and Physics Olympiads, show that I am good at quantitative subjects. I enter the Olympiads because they provide a fun opportunity to apply my knowledge in a different, more creative way. This combination of ability and enjoyment has made my choice of degree easy.

Paragraph 2

[Further reading: detailing specific area of interest and motivation for studying that degree.]
Understanding how people make financial choices is just one of the appeals of this degree. I read Thaler's "Nudge" to gain a preliminary

understanding of how neuroeconomics impacts on this. His ideas were so convincing that I have applied them to myself to improve my planning and action for homework and exam preparation. My generation is experiencing (as Keynes puts it) the "chronic condition of subnormal activity" that is a depression. The waste and suffering of 50% youth unemployment makes no sense if it can be avoided. A deep-rooted interest in tackling this, and in understanding the choices that needed and still need to be made by economists and governments, directed my choice of degree. Krugman quotes Keynes' dictum "The boom, not the slump, is the time for austerity". The opportunity to learn this technical side of economic and business decision-making motivates me. Watching Greece successfully come back to the bond market in April of this year was counterpointed by the fact that on the same day a car bomb was set off in front of the Bank of Greece in Athens to highlight anger against the visit of Angela Merkel, the perceived architect of Greece's austerity. Now more than ever, given the greater complexity of global interaction and the types of exotic financial products available, a close analysis of the choices, costs, and consequences of economic strategy is fundamental to someone looking to contribute to the solutions.

<u>Paragraph 3</u>

[Subject-specific extracurricular activities (Ted talks and EPQ): linking them to show ability to understand context and lateral thinking.]

With the majority of the world now living in cities we face critical choices regarding the allocation of resources. The TED talk "Four

Myths of Urbanisation" highlighted how ghettoes can add value and are to be celebrated or, at the very least, permitted. I went on to explore this in my EPQ with relation to my parents' home city, Lagos, Nigeria. I spent my summer interviewing local politicians and slum dwellers to get as close to the ground information as possible. I am bullish on the prospects for Africa, and particularly Sub-Saharan Africa, despite ongoing internal unrest. The investment and optimism I have seen from the lowest to highest levels is reflected by the business world's growing interest. I was amazed to see there is even a dedicated weekly programme on Bloomberg to the region's changes.

Paragraph 4

[Non subject-specific extracurricular activities (part-time job and drama): providing evidence of organisational skills, determination to go to university, and independence.]
Dealing with sometimes angry customers, taking responsibility for cashing up hundreds or thousands of pounds, and training new staff have been aspects of my waitressing job for the last two years. I took the job as I want to be as financially independent as possible and graduate from university with lower debt than most. Considered by my employers as highly efficient and reliable, I have been offered full-time work in the pub whenever I want, an offer which I will take up this (AS) summer and next. One of the scariest things I ever did was agreeing three years ago to appear in a school play. I did it as I knew I needed to improve my confidence at speaking in public. Acting has given me that and so much more. Since then I have joined a local drama group and passed several LAMDA exams. I am

now even happy to sing on stage. Thinking and working towards a project involving so many others, most of whom do not appear on stage, has given me a real understanding of teamwork and prepares me well for the third year group project in this degree.

Paragraph 5

[Wrapping up: specific offering of that university with reference to career.]

I am highly motivated by the opportunity to learn about [insert aspect of the course] and then apply this in one of the wide range of career directions outlined as options following this degree. I look forward to attending careers events and company visits during my studies. Thank you.

Chapter 11

FINISHING TOUCHES: SPOTTING AND FIXING ERRORS

You are literally a few hours away from finishing your Personal Statement. You have already done most of the hard work: doing the research; deciding on the ideas you want to put across; finding the examples you need to illustrate these ideas; setting the order in which you want to present these; and formulating the words and tone of your statement. All that is left to do is make sure there are no mistakes.

Though there is light at the end of the tunnel, this is not the time for slacking: the final stage is just as crucial as the rest. Waffling on in the first paragraph with descriptions of the course content will lose the attention of admissions tutors. Spilling over the character count because you have listed too many non subject-specific hobbies will lead you to cut valuable and relevant content on books you have read. Letting just one spelling mistake slip into your statement means moving down the list of applicants.

Put simply: this is make or break time for getting an offer from your chosen university. So give yourself time to get it right.

Follow each step below very carefully, and then repeat the process at least once, if not twice.

1. Character count

The first thing you need to do is check that your Personal Statement is between 3,900 and 4,000 characters. Most students constantly check the character count as they go along - at first, because they think they will never have enough to say, and then because they have so much to say they do not know what to leave out.

If you are still over the character limit at this stage, however, you need to make your Personal Statement more concise. There are a number of ways you can rework it to cut down on words.

The main stylistic errors which unnecessarily lengthen your statement are:

(a) Repetition
(b) Too much description
(c) Irrelevant information
(d) Long-winded sentences

Once these errors are weeded out, your Personal Statement is likely to be down to the correct number of characters and make a much more compelling read for admissions tutors. The examples below show you how to tackle each issue individually in your own statement.

****PLAGIARISM ALERT****

Example -- not so good (paragraph 1):

"I am very interested in applying my mathematical ability, which I have proven with my Maths and Physics grades with A*s at GCSE and As at AS, in my future degree and then pursuing a career that will enable me to use it in the real world. I have not yet decided on a specific career path though it is likely to be in finance or finance policy, but I am sure this degree is definitely going to be something I will both enjoy and will give me great skills for whichever direction I eventually choose, especially because of the broad range of modules it offers. The combination of detailed quantitative analysis in the Maths required, research into business and management theory, and pragmatic case studies into real businesses will give me a solid foundation to realise my future ambitions to ultimately pursue a career in finance, just as my brother, father, and grandfather have done."

<u>(a) Repetition</u>

"I am very interested in applying my mathematical ability, which I have proven with my Maths and Physics grades with A*s at GCSE and As at AS, in my future degree and then pursuing a career that will enable me to use it in the real world. I have not yet decided on a specific career path, though it is likely to be in finance or finance policy, but I am sure this degree is definitely going to be something I will both enjoy and will give me great skills for whichever direction I eventually choose, especially because of the broad range of modules it offers. The combination of detailed quantitative analysis in the Maths required, research into business and management theory, and pragmatic case studies into real businesses will give me a solid foundation to realise my future ambitions to ultimately pursue a career in finance, just as my brother, father, and grandfather have done."

Problem:

The idea of pursuing a maths-related career or a career in finance is mentioned three times in the same paragraph. It only needs to be said once.

(b) Too much description

"I am very interested in applying my mathematical ability, which I have proven with my Maths and Physics grades with A*s at GCSE and As at AS, in my future degree and then pursuing a career that will enable me to use it in the real world. I have not yet decided on a specific career path though it is likely to be in finance or finance policy, but I am sure this degree is definitely going to be something I will both enjoy and will give me great skills for whichever direction I eventually choose, especially because of the broad range of modules it offers. The combination of detailed quantitative analysis in the maths required, research into business and management theory, and pragmatic case studies into the real businesses will give me a solid foundation to realise my future ambitions to ultimately pursue a career in finance, just as my brother, father, and grandfather have done."

Problem:

Firstly, you do not need to state your GCSE or AS grades. This information is elsewhere on your UCAS form. Secondly, while it is great to show that you have researched your chosen course before applying, you do not need to regurgitate, at length, exactly what is said in the prospectus. Make reference to it, but keep it punchy.

<u>(c) Irrelevant information</u>

"I am very interested in applying my mathematical ability, which I have proven with my Maths and Physics grades with A*s at GCSE and As at AS, in my future degree and then pursuing a career that will enable me to use it in the real world. I have not yet decided on a specific career path though it is likely to be in finance or finance policy, but I am sure this degree is definitely going to be something I will both enjoy and will give me great skills for whichever direction I eventually choose, especially because of the broad range of modules it offers. The combination of detailed quantitative analysis in the maths required, research into business and management theory, and pragmatic case studies into real businesses will give me a solid foundation to realise my future ambitions to ultimately pursue a career in finance, just as my brother, father, and grandfather have done."

Problem:
That members of your family have worked in finance is not relevant for admissions tutors. If anything, it detracts from your

individual motivation and suggests you are just doing it because everyone else in your family has. Leave it out.

(d) Long-winded sentences

"I am very interested in applying my mathematical ability, which I have proven with my Maths and Physics grades with A*s at GCSE and As at AS, in my future degree and then pursuing a career that will enable me to use it in the real world. I have not yet decided on a specific career path though it is likely to be in finance or finance policy, but I am sure this degree is definitely going to be something I will both enjoy and will give me great skills for whichever direction I eventually choose, especially because of the broad range of modules it offers. The combination of detailed quantitative analysis in the maths required, research into business and management theory, and pragmatic case studies into real businesses will give me a solid foundation to realise my future ambitions to ultimately pursue a career in finance, just like my brother, father, and grandfather have done."

Problem:
All of this paragraph currently lacks punch. The long sentences need to be broken up and interspersed with shorter ones. The repetition should be removed and the thoughts made more concise.

Example -- better (paragraph 1):

"I am yet to decide on a specific career path, but finance and finance policy have a strong appeal. Whichever direction I ultimately pursue, I am sure this degree is something I will enjoy. The combination of detailed quantitative analysis, research into business and management theory, and pragmatic case studies will give me a solid foundation of skills for my professional future."

2. Cleaning up careless errors

You will have read your Personal Statement hundreds of times. This can make you blind to the most straightforward mistakes. Getting someone else (if not two people) to read your Personal Statement at this stage is absolutely essential. They will be able to spot what you no longer can. Make sure to tell them that you do not want feedback on content but instead on spelling mistakes, grammatical errors, and overall use of language.

Errors to look out for:

(a) Repetitive language
(b) Spelling mistakes / homophones (words that sound the same but mean something different when spelt differently - see examples below)
(c) Punctuation errors
(d) Lack of capitals
(e) American spelling

The examples below show you how to spot each of these errors. Follow these and then apply the same process to your own statement.

****PLAGIARISM ALERT****

Example -- not so good (paragraph 2):

“Statistics such as those sighted by Collier in “The Bottom Billion” (50 years life expectancy versus 67 in other developing countries and his analyzing the Four Traps showed me how understanding the underlying causes of socioeconomic issues is the first step to change and improve the lives of many. This showed me that I want to study this degree to gain the basic knowledge and tools to take my interest in economic policy and planning to the next level. My interest lies in economic policy in general, rather than just emerging markets. Reading “End This Depression Now!”, “The Big Short”, and closely following the responses of Bernanke, Abe, Draghi, and Osborne to the global financial crisis (GFC) showed me that, whilst clearly quantitative easing is unsustainable, it was an effective and necessary measure to address the GFC. Writing my EPQ on the currency price movements of four countries (Indonesia, Turkey, UK, and Japan) against the USD since 2007 allowed for extensive research on macroeconomics and market response to economic indicators (eg inflation, GDP, CPI, and PMI) and policy shifts.”

(a) Repetitive language

"Statistics such as those sighted by Collier in "The Bottom Billion" (50 years life expectancy versus 67 in other developing countries and his analyzing the Four Traps showed me how understanding the underlying causes of socioeconomic issues is the first step to change and improve the lives of many. This showed me that I want to study this degree to gain the basic knowledge and tools to take my interest in economic policy and planning to the next level. My interest lies in economic policy in general, rather than just emerging markets. Reading "End This Depression Now!", "The Big Short", and closely following the responses of Bernanke, Abe, Draghi, and Osborne to the global financial crisis (GFC) showed me that, whilst clearly quantitative easing is unsustainable, it was an effective and necessary measure to address the GFC. Writing my EPQ on the currency price movements of four countries (Indonesia, Turkey, UK, and Japan) against the USD since 2007 allowed for extensive research on macroeconomics and market response to economic indicators (eg inflation, GDP, CPI and PMI) and policy shifts."

Problem:
The expression "showed me" is overused. There are plenty of ways round this. Take a look at the suggestions in Chapter 9 for different methods of expression. In this example, you could cut the second instance of "showed me" as it does nothing to enhance the sentence's meaning. In the third instance, you could replace it with "convinced me" and be more specific about how reading that book affected your views.

(b) Spelling mistakes / homophones

"Statistics such as those sighted by Collier in "The Bottom Billion" (50 years life expectancy versus 67 in other developing countries and his analyzing the Four Traps showed me how understanding the underlying causes of socioeconomic issues is the first step to change and improve the lives of many."

Problem:
The statistics were not something that Collier has seen, but information that he has used to prove a point. These were "cited" not "sighted".

Classics to look out for are:

i) your / you're
ii) their / there / they're
iii) principal / principle
iv) complement / compliment
v) effect / affect
vi) who's / whose
vii) sighted / cited
viii) reining in / reigning in
ix) practice / practise
x) license / licence
xi) two / too / to
xii) altar / alter
xiii) ascent / assent
xiv) aural / oral

xv) cession / session
xvi) elicit / illicit
xvii) stationary / stationery

<u>(c) Punctuation errors</u>

"Statistics such as those sighted by Collier in "The Bottom Billion" (50 years life expectancy versus 67 in other developing countries and his analyzing the Four Traps showed me how understanding the underlying causes of socioeconomic issues is the first step to change and improve the lives of many. This showed me that I want to study this degree to gain the basic knowledge and tools to take my interest in economic policy and planning to the next level. My interest lies in economic policy in general, rather than just emerging markets. Reading "End This Depression Now!", "The Big Short", and closely following the responses of Bernanke, Abe, Draghi, and Osborne to the global financial crisis (GFC) showed me that, whilst clearly quantitative easing is unsustainable, it was an effective and necessary measure to address the GFC. Writing my EPQ on the currency price movements of four countries (Indonesia, Turkey, UK, and Japan) against the USD since 2007 allowed for extensive research on macroeconomics and market response to economic indicators (eg inflation, GDP, CPI, and PMI) and policy shifts."

Problem 1:
There is a bracket missing after "countries", closing the bracket opened when referencing Collier's statistics.

Problem 2:
"Four Traps" is a concept you are referring to from a book. This should be in "quotation marks".

Problem 3:
"e.g." is an abbreviation and requires full stops after each letter.

Knowing and spotting this stuff yourself is tricky - so get someone with impeccable grammar to do it for you.

(d) Lack of capitals

"Reading "End This Depression Now!", "The Big Short", and closely following the responses of Bernanke, Abe, Draghi, and Osborne to the global financial crisis (GFC) showed me that, whilst clearly quantitative easing is unsustainable, it was an effective and necessary measure to address the GFC."

You are referring to a period of the recent past which has become a specific term of reference. Capitalise it.

Others classics to look out for are:

i) Prefect
ii) Sixth Form
iii) Mathematics / Economics / Finance / Accounting / Politics (when you are referring to the subject to which you are applying / studying at A-level)

iv) Department (use lower case when talking about a university department in general, but upper case when referring to a specific department) - e.g. “your department’s website”, but “the breadth of the Management Department’s contacts with international businesses”
v) Physics Society / Economics Society (a specific organisation to which you belong)
vi) University (use lower case when talking about going to “university” generally, but upper case when referring to a specific university or mentioning the details of an Open Day you have attended - e.g. “at the Economics Open Day at the University of Exeter”.)
vii) City of London (this is a place name and therefore a proper noun with capitals at the beginnings of the words.)

(e) American spelling

“Statistics such as those sighted by Collier in “The Bottom Billion” (50 years life expectancy versus 67 in other developing countries and his analyzing the Four Traps showed me how understanding the underlying causes of socioeconomic issues is the first step to change and improve the lives of many.”

It should be “analysing”, but better still would be to rephrase this more elegantly as “his analysis of”. You are applying to a British university, so use British English. If you are not sure what is what - check.

i) program should be programme
ii) rigor should be rigour
iii) analyze should be analyse
iv) color should be colour
v) synthesize should be synthesise
vi) honors should be honours

Example -- better (paragraph 2):

"Statistics such as those cited by Collier in "The Bottom Billion" (50 years life expectancy versus 67 in other developing countries) and his analysis of the "Four Traps" showed me how understanding the underlying causes of socioeconomic issues is the first step to change and improve the lives of many. I want to study this degree to gain the basic knowledge and tools to take my interest in economic policy and planning to the next level. My interest lies in economic policy in general, rather than just emerging markets. Reading "End This Depression Now!", "The Big Short", and closely following the responses of Bernanke, Abe, Draghi, and Osborne to the Global Financial Crisis (GFC) has convinced me that, whilst clearly quantitative easing is unsustainable, it was an effective and necessary measure to address the GFC. Writing my EPQ on the currency price movements of four countries (Indonesia, Turkey, UK, and Japan) against the USD since 2007 allowed for extensive research on macroeconomics and market response to economic indicators (e.g. inflation, GDP, CPI, and PMI) and policy shifts."

Chapter 12

TEACHER'S REFERENCE

As part of your UCAS application a teacher at school has to write a Teacher's Reference on your character and ability, and provide evidence of your suitability for the course and for university studies more generally. Typically, the teacher responsible for writing your report will gather mini reports from your different subject teachers, form tutor, and others who know you well, and then consolidate this into a single one page reference.

Unfortunately, not all schools ask students if there is anything they want included, nor do they let them see what has been written. Note that once the Teacher's Reference has been submitted to UCAS, you can request to see it under the Data Protection Act for a small fee.

Teachers will often have to write references for a (very) large number of students. More experienced teachers are likely to know quite a lot about certain courses for which the school's students often apply. They cannot be expected to know or have the time to research, however, the particular features of every course at every university for which their students might apply. Teachers are under great time pressure to get these references written. By proactively finding out which teacher will be writing your reference and by briefing them on the things you think relevant to your application and the course for which you are applying, you will be helping the teacher and making sure the reference you receive is as relevant and strong as possible. In other words, you can help them help you.

Two important pieces of advice:

1. Prepare a briefing sheet

At many of the schools I work teachers find it extremely useful if students provide them with a brief summary sheet. This should include (1) the qualities the university is looking for regarding your specific course and (2) a list of your extracurricular activities (subject-specific or not) and your achievements outside of school. (Teachers may know you, but not well enough to know the details of these.) Concise bullet points work well.

2. Timing

Most universities give out offers on a rolling basis - first come, first served. Many students submit their applications in the second half of the application window. To secure your offers, finalise your Personal Statement and submit your UCAS application early.

Teachers are under a lot of pressure during this period to help everyone who is applying. Avoid the rush by giving your teacher your almost finished draft when you start back in the September of Year 13. If your school does not start the process until Year 13 (this is rare), then get it done as quickly as possible to maximise your chances. This may seem obvious, but so many students delay and delay, which ultimately lowers their chances of getting on their preferred courses or even of getting any offer at all. You can be smarter than them and beat the competition to get your top choice.

Chapter 13

APPLICATIONS FOR JOINT HONOURS

"Joint honours" degrees cover two subjects, either with equal weighting or with one major and one minor subject. University prospectuses will make clear how your chosen degree is set up. Be sure to know this before you start drafting your Personal Statement.

The guidelines for writing a standard, single subject Personal Statement apply equally for a joint honours Personal Statement. The only difference is that you need to be even more selective and concise to ensure you provide adequate evidence of your interest in and aptitude for both parts of the course, along with an explanation of why you want to study them in combination.

The examples below cover the main reasons why students opt for joint honours. Use these to clarify and express your own personal reason(s) for your choice. In my experience, the section explaining this sits well at the beginning of your statement. Throughout the rest of the statement, you must reference both subjects and your interest in their combination through your further reading and subject-specific extracurricular activities.

****PLAGIARISM ALERT****

Reason 1: I love both subjects so much I don't want to give either up.

Example:

"I have thoroughly enjoyed all aspects of both my Economics and History A-levels, particularly the building and analysing of evidence to support theories on why events happen(ed)."

Or:

"How economic events shape history and, in turn, how wider historical events influence economic decisions is fascinating to me because I see evidence of this connection daily in media reports, political decisions, and even in the price and availability of certain foods in the supermarkets. Choosing a joint honours degree was easy, as I wish to give up neither subject and enjoy how they work in combination."

Reason 2: The subjects complement each other to such an extent that the sum is far greater than the parts - i.e. you learn more about each by studying the other.

Example:

"I see the joint honours degree of Accounting and Finance as being symbiotic, in that the understanding of each will give me a better framework for the other. The overlap between the two subjects in both being numerically intense is clear. Wide reading of the course content and comments from current students, however, has shown me that many concepts in both subjects feed into each other in a way that combining the subjects will give me a much more nuanced understanding."

Or:

"Studying Economics and Management together will give me a more rounded understanding of both. I want to know how economic decisions influence businesses (for better or worse) and how businesses should and can respond to changing economic circumstances."

Reason 3: From a career perspective, the two subjects combined give you a greater employability. (This is frequently used when one of the subjects is a Modern Language, e.g. Economics and Spanish.)

Example:

"Choosing to study joint honours in Finance with Management Studies will help me achieve my career objective of working for the finance arm of a FTSE 100 company on their graduate management scheme. As you state on the Faculty website, this degree will allow me exemptions from several professional qualifications and mean that I can progress rapidly in the professional world."

Or:

"After careful consideration, I have decided to take joint honours in Economics and Portuguese, as I want to have a business career which involves work in the Emerging Markets. Studying Portuguese (ab initio) will give me access to Portugal, Brazil, and, most importantly, the economies of several East and West African countries."

(NOTE: "ab initio" is the Latin for "from scratch" and is often used by universities to describe courses which allow you to study a foreign language you have not previously studied.)

REFERENCING EXTRA WORKLOAD

Elsewhere in your statement you must mention that you fully recognise (from your research) that the work involved in a joint honours is significantly more than that of a single honours course and that you have weighed the pros and cons and come to the conclusion that the extra work is more than worthwhile. This often fits well in your final "wrapping up" paragraph.)

Example:

"After speaking to current students on three separate open days I am fully aware of the extra hours of work that a joint honours degree involves. I commit to this willingly as ..."

Or:

"Your website explicitly states how much more is expected of joint honours students. My subject-specific and non subject-specific extracurricular activities (outlined above) show that I have already developed the time-management skills and focus required to handle such demands."

Chapter 14

OTHER HURDLES TO UNIVERSITY ADMISSIONS

Your Personal Statement is finished (well done!), but you have not yet secured a university offer. There is more to come.

Every year at the schools I attend, there are students who have not spent enough time looking at the entry requirements for each of their five chosen universities. Many check only their favourite choice and assume the rest will be the same. This means that they simply do not know about required admission tests, interviews, or submitted work, and, as a result, do not get the results they could have in these because they were underprepared. Read the requirements and give yourself time to prepare.

A few pointers to help you along the way.

1. GCSE Requirements

Many courses have minimum GCSE grade requirements. Every year I meet students who have one or two of their applications rejected without even being properly checked or the Personal Statement read because they selected a university where they do not meet the basic GCSE requirements. If you fall into this trap, you are simply wasting an opportunity. Please check carefully.

2. Admissions Tests

More and more universities are using admission tests (e.g. UKCAT, BMAT, ELAT, PAT, HAT, and TSA) to filter the increasing numbers of high quality students applying. The preparation strategy many students employ is not useful. For tests held in November, students often think that doing minimal preparation over the summer holidays is fine, as they will put in all the hours needed over the autumn half term. This is simply not enough. The best preparation is extensive and enduring, i.e. every day for half an hour in the summer holidays.

The TSA is the test used at some universities for Economics, Management, Finance, etc. Check the link below for full details. Many tutoring services offer focused day-long courses on preparing for this test.

http://www.admissionstestingservice.org/our-services/thinking-skills/

3. Interviews

It used to be mostly Medics, Vets, Dentists, Oxbridge, and Art students who were called to interview, but this is changing rapidly. The use of interviews by universities is increasing even faster than the use of admissions tests. There are many types of interview, from the formal and intense Oxbridge interviews or the multiple mini-interviews (including role playing actors) for Medicine, to the softer “we would like you to come and have a look around the faculty and have a chat” type interviews.

For one-on-one interview preparation, contact me via my website: www.gwynday.com. This training can be done in person anywhere in the world or by Skype, depending on your preference. Alternatively, I work with Oxbridge Applications at several group events around the country each autumn.

4. Submitted Work

This is mainly required by Oxbridge Colleges. If you do need to submit an essay, or in some cases two, there is one vital piece of advice - check the criteria. When doing so be aware of two critical points: (1) the type of essay required (e.g. coursework, a competition essay, an essay written under exam conditions), and (2) the exact type of phrasing required in the essay question (e.g. comparative, textual analysis, summary). Every year I hear from students who have realised too late that they have submitted the “wrong type” of essay and only fully read the criteria on the university website after they have been rejected. You can be smarter than that.

Appendix 1

FURTHER SUPPORT (www.gwynday.com)

The decisions you make during Sixth Form are crucial to your future academic and professional success. I offer a range of one-on-one advice covering Personal Statements, interviews, and future career shaping. If you feel you would benefit from any or all of these services, contact me via my website (www.gwynday.com) to discuss rates and timeframes. This is your chance to stand out.

ONE-ON-ONE PERSONAL STATEMENT COACHING

My Personal Statement Coaching includes unlimited advice, corrections, editing, and proofreading until you are happy with your Personal Statement. As part of the service I offer a money-back guarantee. So if you do not get a university offer, I will give you your money back.

INTERVIEW PREPARATION

I am used by some of the top schools in the UK and internationally to prepare their students for interviews. Taking up my one-on-one Interview Preparation, you can get personalised training. I use the real questions asked in previous years and my NLP expertise to develop your ability to structure, consider, analyse, and, above all, demonstrate intelligent thinking in the pressure cooker that is the interview (or interviews).

THE SIXTH-FORM PROGRAMME

The Programme is specially designed to ensure that you are in the strongest position from Sixth Form onwards to beat the competition. In this process, I help you choose the best course and university for you; guide your further reading and extracurricular activities; tailor university and internship application material to leverage the work you have put in; work with you to prepare for admissions tests; and hone your communication skills for interview. With my guidance, you will be sure to get where you want to go, both academically and professionally, at university and beyond.

Appendix 2

READING LIST

Complete list of the books mentioned in Chapter 5:

"Good Strategy / Bad Strategy" by Richard Rumelt
"Thinking Strategically" by Avinash K. Dixit and Barry J. Nalebuff
"The Bottom Billion" by Paul Collier
"End This Depression Now!" by Paul Krugman
"Nudge" by Richard H. Thaler and Cass R. Sunstein
"The Signal and the Noise" by Nate Silver
"Thinking, Fast and Slow" by Daniel Kahneman
"23 Things They Don't Tell You About Capitalism" by Ha-Joon Chang

Other books to consider (if you have time):

"Capital in the Twenty-First Century" by Thomas Pikkety
"The Worldly Philosophers" by Robert Heilbroner
"Economics" (11th edition) by David Begg, Stanley Fischer, and Rudiger Dornbusch
"Applied Macroeconomics" by Cliff Pratten
"Running the Country" by David Coates
"The First Industrial Nation" by Peter Mathias

"Poor Economics: Barefoot Hedge-fund Managers, DIY Doctors and the Surprising Truth about Life on Less than $1 a Day" by Abhijit Banerjee and Esther Duflo
"The Undercover Economist" by Tim Harford
"Freakonomics" and "Superfreakonomics" by Steven D. Levitt and Stephen J. Dubner
"Accounts Demystified: The Astonishingly Simple Guide to Accounting" by Anthony Rice
"Steve Jobs" by Walter Isaacson
"Titan: The Life of John D. Rockefeller, Sr." by Ron Chernow
"The Everything Store: Jeff Bezos and the Age of Amazon" by Brad Stone

13271524R00108

Printed in Great Britain
by Amazon.co.uk, Ltd.,
Marston Gate.